JN441623

ENERTOPIA

An Affluent Society with Energy

ENERTOPIA

An Affluent Society with Energy

By Jung-ki "Rocky" Park

Translated by Renee H. Park

Carlsbad, CA and Seoul

ENERTOPIA

An Affluent Society with Energy

By Jung-ki "Rocky" Park
Translated by Renee H. Park

First published in 2023
by Hollym International Corp., Carlsbad, CA, USA
Phone 760 814 9880
www.hollym.com **e-Mail** contact@hollym.com

Published simultaneously in Korea
by Hollym Corp., Publishers, Seoul, Korea
Phone +82 2 734 5087 **Fax** +82 2 730 5149
www.hollym.net **e-Mail** hollym@hollym.co.kr

ISBN: 978-1-56591-515-2
Library of Congress Control Number: 2023915003

Printed in Korea

Enertopia is a word that combines the nouns "energy" and "utopia." The Enertopia is a country that generates over 50 percent of its own power needs and does much to encourage the use and the support of energy generation and efficiency.

Prologue

I put my pen to paper again. These are my memoirs from my time as acting CEO of the Korea Electric Power Corporation, or KEPCO.

They say that your predecessors will only learn if you leave instructions, or a play-by-play of your time here. Others say that a memoir may only seem to aggrandize your personal achievements, and serves no purpose. I honestly don't know who is right. They may both be correct.

I turn to my friend, who is a successful businessman. He tells me to please write, because then those who follow in my stead will learn how to think. He makes me promise to only write the truth. I hesitate.

An empty seat may be occupied by anyone. When the established theory is missing, false claims run rampant. If a local convenience store starts selling chemically laden snacks, then it starts harming the children. This is what my friend says. Right or wrong, this story has some truth to it.

I was reluctant. I try to change my mindset. It's doable. After all, I'm just writing the truth, like a real journalist should. But I fear that some may think I'm bragging. I hesitate again.

I am reluctant to receive censure, and yet, I am also afraid of my generation chiding me for not leaving instructions for the younger generations to heed. Fine, I'll write.

I am faithful to the truth until the last. But depending on the reader, there may be spots that they find disagreeable.

I ask for your generosity of spirit in not holding this against me.

Jung-ki "Rocky" Park

Table of Contents

CHAPTER 11 An Exciting Place to Work, A Life Worth Living for: KEPCO

CHAPTER 12 Enertopia

CHAPTER 1

Codes of Conduct

Communication

The heart beats. It pumps out freshly oxygenated blood. The blood circulates, all the way to the tips of the fingers and the toes. The nervous system reacts to the world around it. A person whose blood circulation and nervous system is in perfect harmony—this is an example of a healthy person.

What is the most important factor in a healthy organization? It is communication. The constituents have to talk with one another. The real meaning has to come across, and spread to the heart—then it becomes a healthy organization. What do I mean by communication? Simply put, it is what Koreans like to say; "*Jangguna*," responded to by a "*Mungguna*." It is a call that is answered by another call. This is a "challenge" that has a "response."

So who says *Janggun* first? It is the person who holds the highest office in the company; in other words, it is the CEO or the President. Can anyone just say *Janggun* and expect a rallying response? The answer is a resounding no. To win a game, the call of the hunter, to use an analogy, must be responded to in kind by bloodhounds. The hunter's call, if it is halting or lacking in drive and energy, will issue forth a lackluster response in the dogs, and the situation will stagnate. Please note that I am not saying hard working employees are animals; I am simply using an analogy that may make sense to a Westerner. That is why the CEO must shout *Jangguna*, with certainty; this will cause his subordinates to shout *Mungguna*. Again, this is the pathway to a healthy organization. This is communication at its best, and the way towards achieving a healthy company.

About 50 years ago, former South Korean president Park Chung-hee started the Saemaeul Movement (otherwise known as new village movement). His rallying cry, "Let us live the good life!" was responded to by "the bells toll at dawn." All the citizens of Korea stepped forward, or it seemed like it, back then. This was followed by an export-driven economy, development of heavy and chemical industries, an independent national defense capability, and so on and so forth. To this rallying cry the South Koreans responded. Our sisters' long black tresses, cut and exported with tears (to make wigs), along with fresh graduates from universities traveling en masse to Germany to become nurses or miners, and about 900,000 workers headed to the Middle East, all with the concept of working hard foremost on their minds.

This also marked the entry of South Korea's shipbuilding industry (one of the best in the world), all because we responded to the metaphorical cry of *Jangguna*. We became *Munggun* and followed our president's lead. The excellent communication between the citizens and the country's highest office continued during the Park (no relation of mine) administration, leading to an economic boom for the country.

A leader must issue forth an electrifying call, or a message. That is when his subordinates and other employees will be startled awake. This is the beginning of communicating with one another. The wise all know that *Jangguna* will not just wake the employees' from their slumber. This will make them excited, and they will feel this electrifying energy with their hearts as well as understand and commiserate with their minds. This is why a leader must first shout *Jangguna* impressively. Is this something that anyone can do? This is why not everyone is meant to be a leader, and assigned to be a leader, and try to be a leader.

What defines a great *Janggun*? Please note that *Janggun* can mean, "General," in Korean. A person who makes you see clearly, a person who makes you excited (about work), a person who you cannot help but follow. These are the defining traits of a leader. If you are not on the receiving end of the shout of *Jangguna*, then isn't the fight already over? That is why communication is not with just words. Actions must match your words. In order to do this, a leader must say something that his brethren understand and spur them to action. "Let us live the good life!" is an easy phrase to understand. It's easily applicable. It benefits you. Would you be clumsily timid, or lazy, or just standing there with your arms crossed, when the road to success is so easily explained?

Communication between parties amounts to this: the executive's intent is expressed to his subordinates, and his subordinates are spurred to action by his brilliant turn of mind, and within their ranks, they communicate with one another and their opinions and thoughts are brought over to the aforementioned CEO's attention. These are ideas and actions that circulate and bring a company together.

Communication starts with the leader's message of intent. A message that makes you want to listen, and follow through—this is why a powerful message should be simple and clear. It must be able to be put into action right away. "Let us live the good life!" How clear is this message? And how exciting is this message? Compare it to the stolid "creative economy," or "*changjo gyeongje*." Are they not generations apart in thought? *Janggun*! is a leader who you wish to follow with all your heart, and all your mind, and all your soul.

The Scent of a Human

In late March of 1983, I was issued a message by the South Korean government to head the Korea Electric Power Corporation (KEPCO). At first, I was startled. It was hard enough as is to lead the Korea Heavy Industry and Construction (KHIC), and now they were telling me to become the CEO of KEPCO?!!! I retreated to a small room and fell deep into thought. I couldn't organize my thoughts. From my bookshelves, I selected a book about military science. It was called the "Six Secret Teaching." I just turned to a random page. The first words that I read on that page startled me. "Nothing is better than nothing!" South Korea's biggest state-owned company, KEPCO, could not be used by me to further my own gains, for example, or do as I liked with it; in other words, I had to roll with the punches as they came.

On April 2nd, 1983, an inauguration ceremony was held at what was then the KEPCO building headquarters. Now expensive apartments line the area, on a hill in Samseong-dong. Without a lot of deliberation, I became the CEO. This is really what I would like to call "*muhchaek*," or in this case, without any formal policies or ideas in mind.

After the inauguration ceremony was over, a board meeting took place. Vice President Choi Yeon-sik (Lieutenant General, ROK Army, Ret.), a former superintendent of Korea Military Academy, three years my senior, Prosecutor Shin Dong-sun, and other former graduates of the Korea Military Academy Kim Seon-chang, Mun Hee-seong, Choi Sang-deuk, and Kim Byung-chul (at that time, there was a director system) were present. Outwardly, their attitude was polite but inwardly, they weren't. They weren't going to give in to a "reserve army lieutenant colonel who landed via parachute at a young age." (In Korea, we have a phrase, "*nakhasan tada*," which translates to "arriving via parachute." In other words, it refers to gaining a position—usually pertaining to work, via connections or networking.) To me, there seemed to be only one logical choice. My first challenge was to communicate with them.

From then onwards, I started talking to them one-on-one. I called them to my office, and even broke bread with them. When I met with the technical engineering expert, I tried to listen well. When he stopped talking, I would ask him a question and learn as fast as I could. To teach the CEO is a pleasurable thing, from the other side's perspective. Eventually, when it came to my turn, I would skillfully turn the topic of conversation to management. At the time, I read the works of Peter Drucker and Herman Kahn, which were popular back then. My employees could not help but follow my lead, and listen well. I was leading by example. Before meeting, an executive who was a devout believer of a religion, I would read philosophical works before meeting them in person. For example, when I talked about Calvinism and Puritanism to a person who was devotee of these beliefs, he or she was instantly touched and impressed. It also helped that I had been on the Saudi Arabian peninsula for about five years, and flummoxed at times. Everyone, at the time, seemed to look down on us for not being the top graduates of Seoul National University (SNU), but KEPCO's distinctive style of management required men who had knowledge of the real world, instead of those who only had experience with their noses buried in books. As time passed, these men would come to listen to me, rather than pontificate.

The following anecdote is from a dinner that I had with an executive at a Korean restaurant where I used to frequent, in Samseong-dong. With a passage of time, we opened our hearts to each other.

"How do people see the big boss (CEO) these days?" He broached the subject carefully, then, as if he had resolved to do something, said: "Just hear me out and forget it, sir. They say 'The bastard is a pretty good guy.'"

On this particular evening, we both got drunk.

With all due respect, a person follows not knowledge but virtues instead. What do I mean by virtues? To be honest, I am not exactly sure. Vision, creed, bravery, patience, and other traits like righteousness? Learning, personality traits? Let us just say for now that it is the general aura of the person, or the "scent" of the person.

During a particular era in history, as an individual as well as an organization, there must be some particular issues pertaining to a particular point in time. These small things add up; if you miss the timing, then your descendants will suffer, and furthermore, your nation may suffer as well. To put it bluntly, I believe in a kind of Heavenly will, which is called "*Cheonmyung*," in Korean. There must be a reason why an individual is tasked with a specific line of work at a particular moment in time, and the same goes for organizations as a whole.

If we reorganize people and assign them various tasks, the leader is the one who knows and submits to God's will. Those who live without thoughts will always be the subordinates. It is not a sin to be unable to discern God's will. Maybe it is a God's will for them to live on without understanding what they are meant to live. There are countless other virtues of a human being. But those who understand a God's will for themselves have a certain *je ne sais quoi*. That is why we will always be drawn to people like them. People will congregate around him. This is because he has a certain "scent." To put it mildly, true leadership can only arise from the person who has discerned Heaven's will. Do not what we call virtues stem from people like them?

Let's Walk Energetically!

After the South Korean government assigned me to head KEPCO, I tried to find out more about the company. I also listened to advice from many people. There were many good traits to be found, but at the same time, old evils that had to be done away with. To summarize with a short phrase, the company was, "Giant but like an obstinate old man."

Upon inauguration, I decided to just keep close eyes on how things go for one to two months, instead of doing something immediately. The company's overall mood, habits, and ceremonies seemed conservative, to put it mildly, and when put harshly, I couldn't find any liveliness about it. This is by my personal standards, but to me at the time, it seemed like "a quiet retreat where retirees gathered."

A company without rivals (its strongest asset, yet a type of monopoly) risks becoming an obsolete dinosaur. Indeed, among its strengths were: a steady workplace for life, and a well-paying company. But such a peaceful company without the need for a lot of innovation, like I said before, is privy to becoming stuck in mannerisms.

"The company has to become younger. It has to overflow with energy," I thought. At least, executives in charge of important posts at the headquarter office understand the CEO's mind. The problem was how to communicate with other employees, who were more than 30,000 in number and who were scattered all around the country from the southernmost Jeju Island to the northernmost truce line?

A CEO at the official headquarters in Seoul would not really seem like much of a leadership presence to employees working at the satellite bases, like Jeju Island, or Gangwon Province. So how to reel them in to work towards the company's goals, with me, the CEO, who wanted to innovate the old dinosaur? Somehow, I had to make my presence known, and felt, so that they felt that they were communicating somehow, with the top.

That is why upon accepting this assignment, I decided on making a mission statement with the goal of spurring these far-flung employees to action. This three-point code of conduct included the following:

1) Let's walk energetically.
2) Let's finish today's tasks by today.
3) Let's praise another employee, every single day.

These guidelines are actually direct company orders, in a different sense. This was the first shout of "*Jangguna!*" that I was responsible for. The company entered a state of flux. There were whisperings of discontent, at first. "Does [the new CEO] think that a company is like an army? Just look at this former military officer...I've never seen anything like this [before]." The seeds of discontent were sown quickly and swiftly. They seemed to fester, like a boil. It was as if I had tossed a stone into a peaceful river. An aftermath followed. Out of the blue, this CEO says, "stand up straight with your shoulders back, and walk swiftly…" To most employees that were used to a peaceful workplace, it must have been a shock.

About two months passed. I gathered all the regional heads/branch managers together for a meeting. I spoke the truth. The first impression that I had gathered of the Korea Electric Power Corporation, KEPCO, was this: "[The company was] similar to an arrogant old giant that was stuck in a rut." A workplace is supposed to be a place of winning, a place to take action, and not a place for rest and relaxation, like a vacation spot. Not only this, but as a state-owned monopoly without any rivals, the company must work harder to keep its youthful vigor. In order to do this, we all had to work extremely hard, and put forth great efforts. I reiterated this point; that if these goals were achieved, then it would become saturated by a youthful, vigorous mood. But the catch was this: at first, these may have seemed to be just, orders from the top, but I beseeched the regional heads to make it seem like it came from them, upon returning to their bases. I asked them to put these simple theories into practice.

Meanwhile, every branch, every satellite base, were outfitted with the three-point guidelines that I mentioned before, in order to invigorate every single branch of KEPCO. And every few months or so, I would issue evaluations for them and their progress. During those times, this included those from Jeju Island, as well as Ulleungdo Island. All branches participated. It did not fail, for these three-point guidelines were put into practice. These orders were taken seriously, and every branch realized that it could not put in the bare minimum anymore; we switched on a new system, to use an analogy.

Another two months or so passed. All the branches of KEPCO across the southern end of the Korean peninsula seemed to be injected with a fresh, youthful energy. No more employees loitering or meandering through the halls. No more people walking around with hands in his pockets, slouching. Across the southern peninsula, all the employees of KEPCO at various subsidiaries and the official headquarters in Seoul seemed to now walk with a bounce in their steps. Even those who were initially angry due to the new protocols started voluntarily adopting these measures. It was due to the influence of the others, because finally, finally, it seemed as though everyone at KEPCO was excited to come to work. They could feel the difference in their bodies just by walking with a bounce in their steps and having excellent posture. For these reasons, they were happier and developed a greater self-confidence, with the added bonus of better health.

So Yes, I Had a Drink with the CEO

With the first shout of "*Janggun*!" calling all employees to action, the employees responded with "*Munggun*!" However, there was a slight problem. The problem was communicating with employees in remote areas of Gangwon Province and North and South Jeolla Province. That is why I came up with the idea of hiking. Even on weekdays, I made them go hiking, and called it "*sansang hoeeui*," literally meaning "meetings on mountains." Every time we hiked all the way up to the top, we would hold a simple meeting and discuss the pared down agendas of the day.

I had them hiking up only mountains that were famous, or well known. I limited these one-day hiking trips to about 200 employees, and we selected the right number of people from offices and branches near the mountain we were going to climb. Every weekday, I would travel to a different subsidiary and go hiking with a newly formed group. After the informal meeting, we would go eat together which called "*hoesik*" in Korean. The highlight of this "*sansang hoeeui*" was the group meal that followed the hiking. There was a feast of traditional Korean wine like *makgeolli* and *soju*. This wine-and-dine was to have fun, to boost the participants' morale.

Isn't it a grand thing, to meet the CEO of the company as an employee? The drinks loosened everyone's tongues. I listened, and listened some more. For effective communication, there is no need for long, discursive words. Real communication stems from the heart, from sincerity.

"I had a drink with the CEO today."

This was the phrase used by KEPCO employees back then, when they spoke to their families and fellow employees about these hiking trips. I wonder why I was popular with most KEPCO employees, but not with the regional bosses at the beginning. I, however, began to realize that these hiking trips did not quite please executive level employees who were in their senior years. Perhaps it was because of their age. Besides, some of them had zero experience of hiking, and it must have been quite a toil beyond description.

So I invented this strategy to persuade them with the following words, which was "*sanhaeng odeok*." If it is good for the body, then it is a blessing, if the sound of water flowing in the nearby stream, along with the beautiful vista surrounding you makes you happy, then it is another blessing, if it makes you fall deep into thought it is the third blessing, scaling the mountain all the way up to the peak and admiring the view where it seems like the mountain meets the sky is another blessing, and finally, returning to the Earth and being surrounded by nature while communicating from the heart is the very last blessing. That is why this phrase means, "scaling a mountain, and earning five blessings."

But these mountaintop meetings were not easy for me. From that day, to the next, I metaphorically died a little on the inside. The CEO is like the king, with limited options. There was no drink that I could not accept from my employees. That is why I am thanking the employees who were my dark knights, and helped me not get too drunk. If I had bottomed up all these toasts, I would not have been able to continue these mountaintop meetings.

I love people. I love communicating with them, and hearing their ideas. My love for the people makes me forgive them all, because I was able to turn KEPCO around, back then, to a place where people wanted to work. This is why communication is so important, and yet, so difficult.

Jirisan Mountain

Jirisan is my favorite mountain in Korea. Other mountains such as Baekdusan, Hallasan, Seoraksan are impressive, but for some reason, my heart reverberates with joy when I think of Jirisan. While in Chinese characters, it is called "Jirisan," (or Jiri Mountain), people also call it "Ji-i-san," or "Jirisan," depending on their mood.

Jirisan does not get jealous of Baekdusan's grandiosity nor of Seorak-san's magnificent views. It does not boast, nor does it really have anything to boast about. Instead, it is always comforting, and with a generous spirit, envelops people with a mother-like heart. Do you not like the freedom and generosity of this mountain too?

When we headed off for the mountains for a gathering or event, the most meaningful route was Jirisan. This mountain was the meeting place for employees converging from the Honam area, or about 500, along with about 500 employees from Yeongnam area. Shortly after my inauguration as president of KEPCO, this was the place where I organized the "88 Undong," or "88 Exercise." The number 88 I took from a nearby highway located there.

The 88 Exercise's main point was to mix employees together, and encourage communication, and even marriage between the two locations. We have a phrase in Korea, called "*seonam dongnyeo*," and "*dongnam seonyeo*." The first refers to the men from the west marrying women from the east, and the second refers to the men from the east marrying women from the west. For Gwangju and Daegu, I tried to shatter the long-held divisions between the two provincial cities, and appointed a regional leader who was from the opposite side of town, should I say. So I sent the Gwangju-born and raised Kim Jae-jin to Daegu, and the Gyeongsang-born and raised Park Man-yun to Gwangju. This move at first was met with hesitation. But everyone who was appointed as the regional heads did very well. From the perspective of the regional employees, I am sure some of them grumbled when their new bosses were from a different province that they themselves disliked due to long-held grudges; and yet, this was the beginning of removing fences between neighbors, so to speak.

Chief Kim Jae-jin was a graduate from Korea University, and he was without the usual calculating personality that unfortunately many brilliant men have. He was a kind and generous man, and a man that I would liken to Jirisan. He was one of my favorite subordinates. Park Man-yun, a graduate of Sungkyunkwan University, is another former protégé of mine that I would like to mention. He was tasked with leading the men at the official headquarters in Seoul, and he did marvelously.

I did not just send the regional heads to foreign provinces. Even employees were sent on what I would like to describe as exchange programs, so for about a week or so every month, an employee from Honam would work at Yeongnam, etc. The reason I limited these exchanges to a week was due to them having to relocate their places of residence. So that is why I encouraged home-stays for employees who partook in this program, so cultural exchanges could take place as well. This would prove effective in understanding other provinces and these new understandings, gleaned from experience, and would eventually show in their work upon returning to their assigned offices. These stays were limited to a short period due to another reason: if people are apart for too long, for example, from their homes, then it affects their work. I regret one thing, though; unlike I had hoped, there were not many inter-marriages between the two sides during my tenure.

On May 11, 1985, KEPCO hosted an event called "KEPCO's Southern Rally." I named it like this because I did not like to use the words "*danhap*" (unity), or "*Yeonghonam*" (referring to the Yeongnam and Honam Regions, respectively).

I led the Honam team, and we started at Cheoneunsa Temple. Around 8:00 a.m., we assembled then picked the course from the temple to Sangseonam, Jongseokdae, and Nogodan Peak. The estimated time required would be around four hours. The Yeongnam team was headed by Lee Jong-hun, the vice president of KEPCO. I believe that our hiking trip, which numbered around 1,000 employees in total, must have been the first and the last of its kind. The Yeongnam team chose the following route: assemble at Gurye Dalgung Valley, then hike to Simwon Valley, pass through Imgeolryeongsam Fountain, and finally reach the destination of Nogodan Peak.

The meeting place was Nogodan, and each team was expected to converge at 12:30 p.m. Because of the sheer size and scale of the hiking trip, in addition to it being a rally, a party, and camping trip of sorts, careful preparation was needed. From assembling drinking water, food, and camping equipment for the hikers, our employees who organized the trip really outdid themselves. All the organizers were from the Gwangju satellite office's mountaineering club, while the supervising committee was assembled from the Suncheon office.

The clock finally struck 12:30 p.m. Vice president Lee's Yeongnam team and my Honam team converged at the planned meeting point at the appointed hour. Through our joint leadership, more than 1,000 employees of KEPCO shouted with joy.

"*Manse* (Hurray)!" "KEPCO *manse*!" The employees from the two teams hugged each other. The sight of it moved me deeply. We were as one. There was no you, there was no I. Only the feeling of camaraderie felt between real brethren. I watched this sight with a lump in my throat, afraid that I might tear up at this very real expression of brotherly love between employees.

They say that conflicts can be resolved through communication. I say, the road to communication can be reached in more than a hundred different ways.

How Much Money Did You Receive from the Korean CIA?

In December 1984, I traveled to Japan's Kyushu Prefecture. I was accompanied by Min Kyung-sik, who had just completed his tenure as the head of management at the Kori Nuclear Power Plant. He was one of the founding members of KEPCO's nuclear energy division. He was a man of real character and real skill. His engineering degree from Seoul National University was the icing on the cake, as he had a brilliant turn of mind. He was also well versed in giving reports, or what we like to call in South Korea, "briefings."

Kyushu Electric Power Company and KEPCO shared technology and we were real business partners back then. So it was only natural that back then, there was a real convergence of communication between CEOs, other executives, and employees. We even used to hold baseball matches together, in both South Korea and Japan.

This was when I had a real interest in nuclear energy, so I politely declined the kind Kyushu Electric Power Company's CEO's invitation to visit the spa and tour the area. I asked him instead if I could visit the nearest nuclear energy plant. He readily agreed, and led Min and me to the Genkai 2 Nuclear Power Station, which was in its building phase.

We neared the entrance to the power plant. We unexpectedly met a small group of demonstrators. It seemed as though they were from the surrounding area. It was a sit-down demonstration consisting of around 30 people, and they were an older crowd. I could not contain my surprise and a little bit of suspicion at this sight. I asked a Kyushu Electric Power Company's executive, who had led me and my right-hand man to this power station, and asked him for an explanation. He said they were demonstrating because they did not want a nuclear power plant to be built there.

I was astonished and struck speechless for a while. The Japanese tend to be well mannered and quiet. Another reason for my speechlessness was a nagging fear that the same type of demonstration might happen in South Korea, in the near future. But South Korea was lucky in a sense, because up until that point in our country, there was no real opposition to nuclear energy. But would this be a small taste of what was to come for our country too? I ordered Min to prepare for countermeasures to anti-nuclear power, as soon as we returned to South Korea.

The first step was to appoint Lee Byung-yong, a lawyer and former president of the Korean Bar Association, to assemble an investigative task force. I then sent them all to France. As I have stated before, Lee was a well-known and well-respected lawyer. I needed an executive-level, corporate lawyer in order to deal with potential fallout of establishing more nuclear power stations in Korea. I needed legal and real-time countermeasures.

By that time, France was already relying on nuclear power. About 56 percent of their total energy expenditures came from this source, and they were already planning and building more. But I wondered as to why the outspoken French did not oppose the construction of more nuclear power plants in the country, when the mild-mannered Japanese were actually holding small demonstrations in the middle of the countryside! There must have been a reason, and I was determined to find out what it was.

The investigative task force returned from France with some unexpected news. It was all due to thorough publicity. What do I mean by this? The French government relied on publicity, just compensation, and legal means to back their argument for nuclear power.

With the findings from the task force along with advice from experts in the field, KEPCO came up with comprehensive countermeasures to anti-nuclear sentiment in our country. The man behind all this was Kim Yun-jip, the commissioner of KEPCO at that time.

Kim was a graduate of Seoul National University's School of Law. He was a brilliant man, and the best administrator at KEPCO. I recall him advertising the need for establishing more nuclear power plants in the country during one of the informal mountaintop meetings on Juwangsan.

The main argument behind throwing support behind nuclear power was to continue advertising the benefits of nuclear power to the Korean people as a whole. Out of all the people we targeted, the main target, we decided, was to convince the young people, or namely, university students.

The strategy of public relations became "*baekmuni bulyeoilkyun*," or, "Seeing is believing." In other words, we wanted them to see nuclear power plants in action, and invite them to visit. Targeting the Korean people as a whole involved our subsidiaries to persuade local influential people, and we decided that the head office would host the university students. Convincing the university students would take time-consuming effort. That is why I decided to assign this task to the official headquarters. I also wanted it to be the product of the very talented executive director, Yun Hee-woo. He was another graduate of Seoul National University, and was a genius at planning.

When selecting the students who would be invited to the head office, we carefully curated the ones who were "activists." There were some differing opinions on this strategy, but as I always like to say, it's better to face the problem head on, when the problem is an eventuality.

The field trip was divided into two. The first part involved touring the facilities of a nuclear power plant of KEPCO, and the second part would involve a discussion/debate. The students were invited to the Kori Nuclear Power Plant. They were shown all the interiors, and we explained to them the merits as well as the bad points of nuclear power. The last part of part one of the tour had students dress in protective suits to view the nuclear control room, which was normally a restricted area. For the second part of the tour, we invited the students to the Kolon Hotel, so we could continue the discussion or debate whilst eating dinner.

There had been many questions thus far during the tour of the power plant facilities, but the amount of interest and questions during the debate exceeded the former. I remember the first question. "How much does KEPCO receive from KCIA (now Korean National Intelligence Service) to run this business?" Afterwards, the line of questioning continued along this bias. Luckily, we had the executive director Yun, who fielded questions right and left with aplomb.

Our strategy was to leave no stone unturned. We attempted to address and reassure (student) activists about nuclear energy. We welcomed even the most prejudiced of questions. An odd thing is that if the debate were mostly anti-nuclear power, the more heated the discussion would become, and this really ended up happening, much to our advantage. For there is nothing stronger than the truth.

We held a dominant position during the debate, and the students' fears were allayed. Not only this, but most of them became supporters of nuclear energy. The more we increased the number of field trips, the better the atmosphere became. After dining and drinking beer at a hotel with past alumni who happened to work at KEPCO, all the students' fears about nuclear energy seemed to disappear. Instead, they became fans of the company.

South Korea saw no end of student demonstrations during the mid-1980s. It got so bad that tear gas would prevent us from breathing normally in some parts of the Seoul metropolitan area. However, KEPCO was lucky. Gossip travels fast. Good news about the Korea Electric Power Corporation spread quickly too. Why? Because we held fast to the truth, and explained the importance of national energy needs and nuclear energy as a way to resolve those problems. Their minds responded to our open hearts.

The truth always prevails. Among those many demonstrations and protests, there was not one demonstration regarding nuclear energy. There were no anti-nuclear protests either. Students are in the unique position of learning as much as they can during university, and thus, their understanding is also quick. There was no trickery involved; the truth managed to reach their hearts and minds.

About a year after KEPCO embarked on its PR mission, the Korean Council of University Presidents invited me to lunch. Lunching with the presidents of universities? It was so unexpected that I asked to know more about the event. And guess what. They wanted to give me an appreciation plaque. Why? Because the nature of student demonstrations had changed. Instead of haphazard demonstrations regarding all sorts of things, the demonstrations now were more selective in what they were protesting about. The demonstrations had changed to include rationality. The university presidents wanted to thank KEPCO. To be the guest of honor at such a reception, and be awarded an appreciation plaque, bode well not just for me but also for our company as a whole.

I am a firm believer in upholding the truth; I believe that most, if not all social ills, perceived or imaginary, can be resolved through honesty. Passion and bravery resolve problems as well. If you shirk responsibility, then nothing can be achieved. You must face the problem head on in order to win. The importance of communicating with one another, and communicating well, is something that resonates with me still.

CHAPTER 2

All Employees Promoted by One Rank

One Is 1. Five-fifths Is Still 1.

In military jargon, there is a term called, "momentum of attack." When attacking forces attempt to seize a target and begin their siege, the momentum of attack refers to the strength that the force can hold and endure until the goal is achieved. If they run out of ammunition or troops or fuel, then the momentum of attack becomes weakened. Indeed, it may falter altogether and end in ruination.

Along similar lines, we should keep this term in mind in order to successfully complete a job or mission. We all know there are many good ways to start something. But there are less successful completed missions compared to many promising starts. This is because they lose their "momentum of attack."

So, how to enliven the "momentum of attack?" It has to do with what I would like to call, a "fighting spirit." A rising of morale, if you will. It's like what happens after a downpour; water cascades down a deep valley after heavy rainfall.

So, how to raise morale? You have to excite them. Hearts must speak to hearts. Excite them and get the message across? You have to be generous and come to a mutual understanding. You have to care about them, give them a medal, promote them, and console them, when need be.

Soon after I was appointed the CEO of the Korea Electric Power Corporation, I found that the employees' biggest complaint were their stagnant promotions. Until the early 1970s, new hires resulted in about 500 per year. After 1976, however, for four consecutive years KEPCO hired about 1,500 to 2,000 new recruits. This was due to the rapidly growing energy business. The reasoning was to increase the number of middle management positions. However, since the number of employees was now three to four times that of the past, and had swelled in a short period of time, there was an imbalance that needed to be fixed. Indeed, the management had ended up causing a bottleneck phenomenon, where promotions stagnated, much to the detriment of company morale.

In truth, reaching the level of section chief, called "*gwajang*," in Korean, was about four to five years slower than that of their fellow university graduates who were employed by other companies. Their friends who had found gainful employment in companies with a similar level prestige were already at the very least, "*bujang*," or department heads, or "*isa*," or company directors. It hurt KEPCO employees' feelings, as well as their pride.

It's worth noting that for white-collar workers, the promise of better pay and a promotion often go hand in hand and are sometimes even a matter of life or death. Additionally, promotions, or lack thereof, impact the world of human relationships. Imagine going to an alumni event and passing around business cards. The guy who had always had not much going for him now has the title of "head of department," or "director," and you turn away from self-shame and an embarrassed wife, who is tugging at your sleeve. Metaphorically speaking, of course. This sense of shame must have been very difficult to endure.

When this problem came to light early on during my tenure at KEPCO, I myself felt badly for all of them. "Yes, I will resolve this issue for them," so I thought. I meant this sincerely, with all my heart. I called the head of management/human resources, and urged them to quickly find a solution to the issue of stagnating promotions. I did my part too. I searched for solutions myself. Oh no! Maybe this was a problem without a solution. Many days passed, without a single word from the head of HR.

I knew that the executive directors might not have a solution to the problem. It doesn't make sense to hire four or five times the right number of people and then promote them normally.

Many days passed, yet again. The solution that they finally brought to me was very long and complicated. But in all honesty, there was no solution. And rightly so. I had ordered my employees to find a solution to a problem that may not have a solution. So what was the solution that they finally brought to me? They wanted to expand the organization, reorganize the company, and make room for more (employees). What nonsense was this! Or so I thought. This strategy was impossible to implement, and rightly so. It was a classic case of "*wi-in* seolgwan," or making extra room for increasing recruitment, which had caused the problem of stalled promotions.

I am sorry to say that when I was assigned to head the Korea Electric Power Corporation, I saw the need to streamline the company and the employees. Three years prior, when I was the CEO of the Korea Heavy Industry Corporation, one of the first things I did was to cut the number of executives by half. This was the problem that I saw back then, in government-owned companies; obese corporations that needed to slim down in order to be more effective.

Did I have selfish motives in wanting to slim down KEPCO? Of course not. I had a plan coming in, and things were not going in the direction of the original plan. Instead, they chose to increase the size of the company by hiring more employees! At the very least, this move would violate my vision for KEPCO.

But then again, when I thought of the employees who were hurting, my heart hurt too. But what to do! Should I abandon the problem of stagnating promotions? Or force them to find a different solution? Something that doesn't work will never work. I felt like I was between a rock and a hard place. I lost my temper. I worried about this problem for several more days. I worried and worried some more, while sleeping and while walking.

I remembered a wise saying from Peter Drucker. "Delaying a decision is [sometimes] an excellent decision." Maybe I would do this too. It was a difficult choice that I made, because I hate delays. But this was the only way back then. But then, a strange idea passed through my mind. How did Drucker come up with such a sphinx-like solution? It's like the Arabic numbers, and the genius who came up with the idea of "zero." Maybe this quote was an inspiration from the man who thought up "zero."

It's the real number, "zero" which takes up the very center stage, though it's neither plus nor minus. A glass is half empty versus a glass is half full; somewhere between pessimism and optimism, a neutral value. Not making a decision was a decision in and of its own, a solution of its own, and was this not a fantastic idea? Then suddenly, I was struck by a novel idea. "1 is 1. 5/5 is still 1. 100/100 is still 1. Then should I specially promote all the employees? 100/100 or 1/1 still has the same value as 1. If I just change what it's called, the original '1' would not change, and since the original essence is not changing, then the organization or the current balance of it all would not change." Since everyone would be promoted, no one would nurse a stomachache (the latter of which is part of a Korean saying).

"Aha!"

I called the heads of management/HR to my office.

"Number one. A section chief is now a manager, a manager is now a general manager, and a general manager is now the chief of the department. Change their titles so they advance one level. Number two. There is to be no change within the organization, such as reshuffling or reorganizing, or adjusting other positions. Number three. The salary remains the same until next year's promotion. I myself will seek the government's understanding."

The head of management as well as the head of human resources looked confusedly at one another.

"Just do as I said. I will shoulder the blame [should anything bad happen]."

After a few days, every branch of KEPCO was issued these orders. The human resources department inadvertently leaked some of these secrets accidently, in implementing these orders. But the message was clear; when the employees were made aware of these changes, it seemed as though there was a roar of appreciation that I could hear from all the way in Seoul. A special promotion for all! Numbering over 20,000 men and women! It was unheard of. There is a saying in Korean that Hanyang's paper prices cost more than the news that are printed on them, but one of the gutsy executives said to me then, "President Park, the nation's printing presses have run out of paper." What on Earth was he referring to? The need for new business cards for everyone.

This special promotion for all was like a megaton nuclear explosion. It seemed as though KEPCO would burst with joy. I say now, that the country did not run out of just paper; they must have run out of alcohol, as well.

I recollect visiting one of the satellite branches after this special promotion. One of their managers then said to me, "President Park, thank you. I do not know how to thank you for your kindness."

It was an awkward moment for me, so I said in response: "How can you say that to the CEO of this company? Within company grounds?" I was half-joking, of course.

But he immediately said to me with a serious face, "I have a daughter who is getting on in years, and due to this promotion [of mine], she was finally able to get married." My heart zinged.

Even after this, there were exciting tales, and comedic tales, and delightful ones, that I had the pleasure of coming across. For several months, KEPCO seemed to have lost its desultory manner.

That year, did not the unofficial catchphrase become, "KEPCO, an exciting workplace, and KEPCO, a workplace worth living for!"

CHAPTER 3

Executive Secretary Lim Chang-geon

Bitter to the Mouth, Better for Your Health

When you become the top brass, it's good to have firm supporters. Be they supporters from your hometown, school, or elsewhere, a good leader will have a circle of supporters he can rely on, no matter what. I digress, but what harmed the leadership of former South Korean president Park Geun-hye was the lack of firm comrades and supporters like so called "*Donggyo-dong*," (supporters of former South Korean president Kim Dae-jung), or "*Sangdo-dong*," (supporters of former South Korean president Kim Young-sam).

But then again, when I was first appointed chief executive officer of the Korea Electric Power Corporation (KEPCO), I worried a bit. I did not expect firm supporters at KEPCO. In the early days, the bit that disheartened me the most was the lack of a network that would be my eyes and ears during my tenure.

How could I know if all the satellite branches of KEPCO were running smoothly? Back then, there were about 400 such places of business that were somehow tied to KEPCO. How could I know if my decisions were being disseminated properly at each, and if the reports that I was receiving from everyone were true, even down to the very bottom rung of the corporate ladder?

As the last resort, I drew to the conclusion of utilizing alumni of the Korea Military Academy, as there were about 20 of them at the company. From time to time, I called on meeting with them to hear the real, behind-the-scenes stories of the rank-and-file hierarchy. The alumni, who were juniors at the company, however, did not report anything helpful. They all said that everything went well and everyone was good. I complained to them then, saying that I did not want fans parroting praise, but real-time, real-life reports on how the company was operating. But these several meetings ended with me just becoming frustrated more than ever.

But one day, much to my surprise, one of the quietest alumni from the Korea Military Academy, who had been sitting in a corner, raised his hand. He was a quiet lad, who was a member of the KMA Class of 1968. Lim Chang-geon, was his name and he was a section chief, or "*gwajang*."

"Yes, do you have anything good to report?"

"The last order you issued was one of your worst commands ever." He just threw that out there, without an explanation.

"How so?"

"It doesn't fit with the day-to-day workings of the company." We all turned our heads to look at this upstart young fool (or so we thought). The ones who had graduated before him, a graduate of Class of 1959 and a graduate of Class of 1961, looked deeply aggrieved.

"What do you mean it cannot be executed properly?" I asked him. I myself started becoming cross.

His explanation was brief, but it had some merit to it. While what he was saying was reasonable, it hurt my feelings. At first, I thought to myself, “This guy is just too young to preach me. How dare he says something was wrong with one of my decisions?” I hate to admit it, but humans are truly foul beings sometimes. I had gathered my alumni for a meeting, to hear the truth, and yet, I became cranky upon discovering that something was amiss. How ironic.

As soon as the meeting was over, I sat in the backseat of the company car, and reassessed my situation. My anger dissipated somewhat. The grim reality that Lim was right was a bitter pill to swallow until I had retired for the night.

After that, I only called Lim to the office for these meetings. I did not need all the alumni there. His reports were precise and on-point. There were meetings where he said more bad things than good, usually. I decided then that I would call him my “executive secretary.”

One day, Lim came into my office with a very serious expression on his face.

“So, he’s got another bad report, has he?” thought I as I moved to my desk. There are no lounge chairs in my office.

“What? Do you have another good report for me?” I asked.

I was joking, of course. I had grown somewhat accustomed to his somewhat caustic reports. He didn’t talk right away. He let me stew for a little while, which is odd for him. Lim wasn’t acting like himself, and that worried me. A little.

“What! Tell me!”

“I am sorry, this is something personal…”

“What?”

“I cannot believe this bloke has come to me with some bad personal news," I thought to myself.

"So what is it?"

"Do you know what my job is?"

"What kind of absurdity is this? There are over 3,000 managers like you at [this company]. How can I, the CEO, know what you are in charge of?" I thought.

"So stop beating around the bush. Let's have it."

I could not stop my jaw from dropping to the floor at his words. According to Lim, there was an unfair contract he's been working on for seven years, and it has been making the company lose millions each year. But instead of seeking a solution, the company has been avoiding the problem day-by-day, year on year. This wasn't the only bad news. Everyone was avoiding the problem like the plague, and if someone didn't find a solution soon, the problem would snowball until it collapsed upon itself, causing ruin. I could not believe my own ears. Under broad daylight such a thing was happening!

"What? How could such a..."

I was as speechless as I was surprised. I didn't understand what he was saying.

"Ok, boy. Say it slowly."

I could not believe the words coming out of Lim's mouth. In 1969, about fourteen to fifteen years ago, KEPCO had contractually entered into an agreement with Kyung In Energy; but because of some details of this very contract that did harm the KEPCO, the company was bleeding at least 10 billion Korean won every year (about $24.8 million U.S. dollars by today's estimates for a total of about $372 million U.S. dollars).

"So before I became the CEO, for over 10 years, they have known about this, but haven't done anything about it?"

"Yes."

"The previous CEOs have known about this?"

"Yes."

"And we will lose another 10 billion won this year?"

"Yes."

"If you keep saying, 'yes, yes,' do you call that an answer?"

I lost my temper then, much to my chagrin. Unfortunately for Lim, I lashed out verbally at him.

When I finally learned the whole story from him, I was simply astounded. Kyung In Energy was established by the Hanwha Corporation and the United States' Union Oil, with each getting a 50 percent stake in the company. At the time, the head of the KCIA's special plea led to an unfair contract. The CEO then was Jung Rae-hiuk. I heard an anecdote that after signing the contract, he drank a whole bottle of Johnnie Walker Whiskey. This seemed like some kind of horrendous (South Korean) drama, as told by Lim.

While manager Lim was finishing up his tale, I finally regained my senses and my rational mind. I decided to ask Lim to summarize his current duties and come up with possible countermeasures, and have him report back to me as soon as possible.

The best countermeasure was to renegotiate the contract. The problem was that Kyung In Energy was loath to do this. According to commercial law, a mutual agreement that benefited the other party and was otherwise legal would not be given up easily by the said party.

"This is unfortunate. This is a problem that can't be solved through conversation, so doesn't that mean we have to use force?" I thought.

I immediately gathered all the executives to renegotiate. The renegotiation process was long and arduous. It was not smooth sailing at all, and it was more of a "sit it out" kind of situation. It was one of my lowest points during my tenure. I did not want to take this path. I was in the right, and there was no need for me to get out the big guns. I wanted a contract that was reasonable, and wanted to settle it quickly. Tough negotiations ensued, but without a solution; day-by-day, the fight got bigger and bigger.

It goes to show that when negotiations escalate between companies or even in human relationships, it can lead to catastrophe or both parties becoming harmed. Escalation happens when one party digs their heels in and disregards reason. From a reasonable point of view, this is a stupid way to be. But this is a part of being human. This renegotiation was no different.

With no promise of a new contract in sight, things reached a critical point, then burst. I wonder now if my inability to make them see things rationally contributed to this. But at the very last, I realized that I needed, as I mentioned before, to resort to a last countermeasure; resort to the big guns, if you will. I am sorry.

A show of force is a type of military action. It must be short, brief, and decisive. It has to be a direct hit, an all-or-nothing type of action. This act also protects both parties from more harm.

I asked them what the KEPCO's strongest move might be. It was to cut off the pipelines so that they couldn't run generators. I immediately ordered the employees to shut off the valves. The bosses stared at me in shock. They thought it was too aggressive a move, certainly. There was no room for the other party to even retreat, no mouse hole for them to scurry to. That's not true, though. Giving the other party an escape route was absolutely out of the question, as it would hurt the company and me. At a point like this, there was no room for hesitation.

"Shut off the oil pipelines tomorrow. No exceptions." I said this forcefully.

Early on the next morning, as I was getting ready for work, there was a phone call for me from the Hanwha CEO's office. He wanted to meet with me directly. Shutting off the valves must have caused chaos over there, I thought to myself. I wondered why we had to have come to this point, and success tasted bitter in my mouth. I knew that inviting him over to my office would not be right. Instead, I decided to invite him to dine with me at a small Korean restaurant in the Mapo district.

CEO Kim Seung-yeon. He's young. He's a cool guy. He's brave. I liked the way he spoke. It was refreshing, like a cool summer breeze. He says, let's do it your way. He says that he doesn't even have any conditions that need to be met, and likewise, he says that I must not have any either. On my part, I say, let us return so that work commences. Let us make the contract a win-win for both companies. This rationale works magnificently. The world may see him differently, but I see him as a good man.

I felt this whilst talking with him, but I wondered if he was too scary, and if this was his Achilles' heel. He seemed not to understand the heart of the problem. He must not have had his subordinates report back to him with real-time data, or with problems. Because he was too scary. As of this writing, his advisors must have been skirting the scary issue because they were too afraid of the big boss, and this catastrophic turning of the valves must have happened because they were too afraid to tell him the truth. If you see the heart of the problem and report back on it, and get a decree on how to commence, then it will not lead to catastrophe. When you are afraid of your boss, you try to hide this way and that, and then it can lead to horrifying consequences. When you become CEO of a company, your outlook changes. It has to be different from that of your subordinates. If you receive the good news as well as the bad, then it is up to the CEO to make the correct and the most reasonable decision.

Let me digress for a moment. More than 10 years ago, I wrote a book titled, *Stories of Leadership*. In the book, I write about something called "*daegwan*." I cobbled two Chinese characters together. It is not in the dictionary. It's a word that I have invented. It means "great generosity." It's common for bosses to want their subordinates to report back on things good and bad, but in reality, this is hard to put into practice. If you report back on problems, for example, then you might earn the disgust of the CEO and end up blocking your way towards advancing up the career ladder; who on Earth would risk his career to report on things both good and bad? This is not something that we must expect from a subordinate. Instead, we should expect it from the CEO. He must behave well himself.

If you become the head of a company, it is my personal belief that he should be personable, so that a generosity of spirit permeates from him and that his leadership is tempered by this trait. This means that he must be open to both good as well as bad reports, and that his subordinates should not be frightened to come to him to talk.

One day, a laborer at a farm comes and complains to his boss, Hwang Hui. Hwang Hui says to him, "You are right," and turns around, and another farmhand comes to him with a different story, contradicting the one he has just heard. He listens to the whole tale, and then says to the second day laborer, "You're also right."

Hwang Hui's wife, who has been listening all along, says to her husband, "Dear husband, how can both be right?" Hwang Hui replies, "Dear wife, you are also right." This famous story from Korean history turned folklore demonstrates "*daegwan*." This is why he loyally served three kings, or so they say.

Prime Minister Hwang Hui, famed for serving three kings, is not saying these words cryptically on purpose. They are all right, depending on which perspective you are viewing the problem from.

We reached an amicable settlement. A win-win for both of us. It was like KEPCO had pulled out a festering tooth that had been rotting for almost 20 years. But I nursed a small regret. Had former incumbent Hanwha President Kim Seung-yeon understood the concept of "*daegwan*," then we could have prevented the company from bleeding millions. This was back in November 1985.

I would hear later from sources close to department head, or "*bujang*" Lim (because of the special promotion for all in October 1984, he was also promoted by one rank), how the other side kept on trying to buy his silence by offering him a large-sized apartment and cash amounting to 100 million Korean won. Of course, since I did not hear it directly from him there is no sure way of knowing, but knowing Lim, I sincerely believe that such bribes would not come to pass. There is a phrase, "even if there is a knife in one's throat." Lim was that kind of fellow. He was a man that I trusted entirely.

The next day I called one of the assistant directors of the human resources department, Cho Jae-gang, to my office. He was a graduate of the Korea Military Academy Class of 1961. I told him to immediately promote Lim to another position. Another promotion by one rank, if you will. Because of the promotion, Lim would no longer be reporting to me directly to my office. It was decided that he would become the vice branch manager of the Incheon branch.

A few days later, I called Cho to my office.

"I wish to use Lim as my chief assistant executive…"

"Dear President Park, I cannot assign that role to him."

"What? It can't be done?"

"That particular role can be assigned to a person who holds the Rank 1 status."

"Well, I don't understand!" I became cranky.

"It's in the company regulations, sir."

In the book of complicated company regulations, Cho knew the rules, and what the role of chief assistant executive would consist of.

"Bring me the company regulations!" The company regulations stipulated what Cho had told me about. I fell into deep thought. I really wanted to change these regulations so that Lim could serve in this position. An uneasy silence followed.

"Even if you have to fix the rulebook, make sure that Lim holds this position!" I said finally with triumph.

Cho stared at me. On his face, was an expression of disbelief, like he was saying with his face, "No way!" My face must have seemed frozen. He left my office without another word.

A few days passed. Cho brought me the new rulebook. The previous rule that limited Rank 1 alone should be assigned to the role was revised. Now, it said "Rank 1 or 2 can be assigned." The person in charge of the revision worked his or her brain. So this was how I celebrated the birth of a great chief of staff.

Lim had graduated from Korea Military Academy in 1968. Upon arrival at a frontline unit as a platoon leader, he had been committed to a mop-up operation against the North Korean guerrilla atttacks in Uljin and Gangneung. Unfortunately, Lieutenant Lim had stepped on a landmine and had sustained injuries. Because he had been moved to the first-rank veteran retention system, he was able to find employment at KEPCO. This accident had led him to me.

During my entire tenure as the CEO of KEPCO, he never disappointed me, not even once. All the time, he looked at a problem from a different angle, and when he was opposed to my viewpoint, he would not hesitate in expressing his views. He was not right all the time, of course, but this contrary point-of-view, if you will, made up for my faults and preemptively stopped mistakes. When I look back on it, there are many things to be thankful for. Lim, and the rest of his team, were all great men. Chung Dong-rak, Lee Do-sik, Lee Gil-gu, I count as among the finest in the line-up.

Of those still remaining at KEPCO, include Son Tae-kyung, a graduate of the ROTC and of the same recruiting class as Kim Mun-kyung. He was a great speaker of French. He was an overseas employee for a while, and he was the one who fixed the fiasco over the chief of audit and inspection, Korea Hydro & Nuclear Power Co. Ltd. back in the day. He is now the head of purchasing. Huh Kyung-goo, who had received an MBA from George Washington University, and had worked at the New York satellite office, is now the head of the overseas business division. Ha Hee-bong, who joined the company in 1985 as one of the top recruits, was one of those who did not want to serve in the secretariat, even against my direct orders as CEO. He had a peculiar reason for not wanting to serve in this post, so I "forgave" him. He wanted to be a real KEPCO man, and thus wanted his post to be in one of the regional offices at first. Everyone else, for the most part, wanted to stay in Seoul but he wanted to serve at a regional post first. He was a strange one. But we acquiesced to his wishes. His first post was in the remote area of Sancheong, then moved to Jinju as the Jinju branch manager. He is now the Director of Materials. All are men fit to serve as CEO. They are truly first-class men. The attending secretary, manager Cho In-guk, was another strange one. "He who follows like a shadow," is a similar connotation, but a shadow leaves a mark. Sometimes, it can disturb. The hallmark of a good employee in the secretariat division means that he must be like an invisible man, assisting without delay without drawing attention to himself. Young as Cho was, he knew this. In the future, he would become the vice president of KEPCO, and currently serves as the president of the Korea Western Power Corporation, Ltd.

Even now, I think of Lim and Cho in the highest esteem. Even after my tenure, whether or not I was feeling strong or weak, they spent a lot of time with me, and were loyal to the last.

CHAPTER 4

Hanil
General Hospital

Vice Premier Shin Byeong-hyun

The now defunct Hanil General Hospital, located in Seosomun-dong, opened in 1954. It is a hospital steeped with history for me, and especially KEPCO. Until May 1988, when it moved to Ssangmun-dong, it used to be a hospital affiliated with the Korea Electric Power Corporation. It played a large role in treating KEPCO employees for various ailments, and especially those suffering from electrical accidents. For us, it was a hospital that we could not be without. But because we were a state-owned corporation, and because of the government's decree that non-essential facilities and subsidiary companies be sold, the hospital too, was sold, shortly after I started my tenure as CEO.

When I started as CEO at KEPCO, all the employees wanted to keep Hanil General Hospital. Not only was the hospital easy to use, but the treatment fees as well as the admission fees were reasonable. The more I thought about it, I thought it should still be seen as a part of the employees' benefits package and that the hospital itself should not be sold.

At first, I consulted with the Energy Minister. He said he could not help, because the government had already decided to scrap the partnership. I then went to the Economic Planning Board. Again, a resounding no. They said to me, "don't work so hard for the impossible, and make early preparations to accept our plans."

So who did I go to next? Shin Byeong-hyun, the Minister of Economic Planning. He had already served as the Governor of the Bank of Korea and as the Minister of Commerce and Industry. He was a man nearing 70. I thought maybe he might listen, and be willing to talk.

"Vice Premier Shin, isn't the point to sell off subsidiaries that are reporting a deficit?"

"Yes."

"What if I put them in the black?"

"Well, that couldn't be done, so that's why we're doing this instead."

"Well don't you have to see whether the hospital will be in the red or the black before making a decision?"

"Before you came, CEO Park, it had already been decided upon. How can we change already laid plans?" He seemed cantankerous.

"That is why I am here to tell you that that decision was wrong."

"What? How much do you know about the running of a hospital?"

He seemed to think, "what a stubborn fellow."

The running of a hospital and its management are even more complicated than a hotel. If it is to be in the black, then the number of occupied hospital beds must be above 250, but Hanil General Hospital is at 150, he said. He seemed to know it like the back of his hand.

At about this time, one should retreat. But I was also at my wit's end. The truth was I had promised my employees that I would save the hospital for them; I had given them my word. Not only this, but I myself thought that we needed Hanil General Hospital. The problem was that I had not known the government would take such a hardline stance, and I had tried too quickly to resolve the problem.

"So if I make [the hospital] operate in the black, then wouldn't the problem be resolved?" This question just popped out of my mouth.

The Vice Premier stared at me quizzically.

"You may not know how a hospital operates, but you know about businesses. So how can a businessman say such a thing?" I felt a small sense of humiliation creeping in.

"I will make sure the hospital operates and turns a profit." I decided to match his hardline stance with that of my own. The Vice Premier looked at me, at a loss for words.

"Ok. Stop for today. But I am warning you, this is an impossible thing you have promised." He stood up from his seat.

His manner meant that he would not give me more time to talk. My words did not sink in. He was a wall made of stone, metaphorically speaking. I knew that the police hospital was also being sold off. According to rumors, the police force were also very upset by the selling off of their hospital, and resisted as long as they could, until they were literally forced to sell.

That is why I couldn't force his hand for KEPCO. For the South Korean government, the eventual selling of the Hanil General Hospital was a sure thing, and they were tired of hearing otherwise. I had not known this, and I was somewhat hasty in my quest to save it.

But retreat now? No, I couldn't, and I wouldn't. My steely resolve may have seemed ungentlemanly, but it was for the good of the company, and I had the best of intentions—I decided to go as far as I could. Another reason for my stubbornness regarding this matter was the difference between Hanil General Hospital and the police hospital's business and other matters. Hanil General Hospital was a special hospital, even if its name indicated otherwise. It was a place to treat electrical accidents, which most hospitals did not know how to treat. If I may speak boldly, the police hospital could be sold, but the specialized practice of Hanil meant that in my view, it shouldn't be sold at all.

I decided to butt heads. I knew that it would not be an easy task. I made a chart. This was before the development of Power Point presentations. I asked for a face-to-face meeting several times, and was turned down several times. I finally got a small reprieve in that the Vice Premier agreed to see me again. I was filled with a sense of purpose.

"So, you come to me again with the same problem?"

I stayed silent and just opened my chart.

"A chart? Better not waste your energy. Why don't you stay for a cup of tea instead?"

I stayed silent and prepared to give my argument. My firm attitude must have surprised the Vice Premier, for he said then, "Fine, let me see what you have prepared."

"I am going to resign as CEO unless Hanil General Hospital is in the clear." I had written only these words.

I had avoided topics such as why it shouldn't be sold, why Hanil General Hospital was necessary, etc. The Vice Premier stared at me. I deliberately did not waste any words. This is the work of the Holy Spirit; the work cannot be done with mere words.

A long silence followed.

"I'll see you in three months."

Heart spoke to heart. This type of unspoken brotherhood that flows between men, is this not the work of the Lord?

Vice Premier of finance, Shin Byeong-hyun, was born in 1921 in Hwanghae-do Province. He earned his Ph.D. from Columbia University in the City of New York. He served in the role of the financial planning minister twice. His nickname is "Gom Ba Whi," which roughly translated, means "Stone Bear." During the Fifth Republic in South Korea, where military pressure was exerted, he was an excellent defender of the country and was a high-spirited fellow of deep convictions. He passed away in 1999, at the age of 79. I regard him highly even today.

"This is the work and the decree of the government. It cannot be done." He could have rejected me thusly. But he gave me a fighting chance, and I took it. But he issued me a warning of sorts. He said, "Well? If you plan to do that, then I am willing to watch over you for a few months, okay?" How wise he was!

So now I was in a bit of a bind. The ball was in my court, but my position as CEO was now in jeopardy. Of course, there would be no way to make the hospital profitable in a few short months. The Vice Premier would indeed, wait and see me for three months.

Noh Tae-il, Chief of the Department

Upon returning to my office, I tried to organize my thoughts. I had not expected the Vice Premier to agree with me so readily. In actuality, this problem had already been resolved, from the point of view of the South Korean government. The decree had been passed already. That is why I knew that from the onset, I would need to overcome several obstacles in my path, and success seemed futile, at best. But I had met someone, a gentleman, who increased my chances slightly by buying me more time.

"Okay, let's do this," I said to myself.

I immediately went into investigative mode, to figure out the actual conditions of Hanil General Hospital. As I had feared, they had fallen into a type of management without a sense of firm purpose or ownership. This is what we call "mannerism" in the hybrid language of "Konglish." Every single year, the Korea Electric Power Corporation would give it about 2 billion KRW, to make up for the deficit. It was not a place to "vacation" at; rather, it was more like a "nursing home." The hospital did not seem to want, or were too overwhelmed, to fix the problem. I hate to say this, but my first impression when I actually visited was that the hospital was disintegrating, and that it should have been shut down long ago.

I went to the hospital director's office. At the time, the head of the hospital was a former brigadier general who had served as the Surgeon General of the ROK Army. One question levied at him was enough.

"Do you believe that you are the owner of the hospital?" This question went beyond just learning and basic human dignity. He seemed to regard the post as an assignment only. This is the problem with most working men who rely on a salary. I did not need to speak to him for a long time. The next day, I requested that the hospital director be dismissed. I was sorry, but only from the perspective of a fellow man, and not as a boss.

So then, who to bring in to fill his shoes? I asked around the hospital for recommendations. It was not easy. Days passed without a hospital director, for there was no one worthy enough. During those times, it was rare to have someone without a medical degree to serve as a hospital director. I changed my mind. Did the new person need to be a doctor? Is it necessary to find a person from outside the organization? I just needed someone who would be like the CEO of the Hanil General Hospital and care for it as if it were his own. And another quality I was looking for was intelligence.

I decided to limit the pool of candidates to the current organization. An expert can fill a position that needs specialized training. But I ran into a problem. Would the hard-nosed doctors and nurses listen to a director? How would the medical community respond if it became one of the first hospitals to have a non-doctor become the new head of Hanil General Hospital? Not only this, but the government was already looking for another candidate to fill my shoes. I had risked my own position as CEO of KEPCO to get the hospital to turn a profit, instead of reporting losses, every single year. I had to find a really talented person. This person ideally would have a noble mien, ability, as well as good physical attributes. This is because the patients would need to be reassured too. It was a difficult Human Resources problem.

For several days, I looked at the roster of directors at KEPCO, and did some sleuthing. It would be hard to find someone who met all the qualifications I was looking for. I worried over this for several more days. At the end of my own deliberations, I picked one from the roster. It was the chief of the department, Noh Tae-il. He was tall, around 186 cm, had excellent posture, and a face resembling that of Buddha. Not only this, but he was a man of intelligence and ability.

The very next day, I called director Noh to my office. I told him curtly that the problem of Hanil General Hospital was one that involved KEPCO. There was no need for long explanations. I spoke plainly and truthfully. "If you do not take this position, there is no one as qualified as you are to serve as the new head of the hospital." Upon hearing this, Noh's face turned ashen. For a while, a heavy silence hung in the air.

"President Park, I would rather resign."

I was at a loss for words. It was as if a lightning bolt had suddenly struck me. On a personal note, I was sorry. To put one of my own executives who were well on their way towards achieving even more dizzying heights up the career ladder, this move would seem like a step backwards, or even several. It wasn't a cherished position either. But from my view, there was no one other than Noh to fill the prior head's shoes. The heavy, uncomfortable silence continued.

"Fine. Let us talk again tomorrow," I said. We both became uncomfortable. In a situation like this, it is best to avoid each other.

The next day, I did not look for Noh. I did not call him to my office. I wanted him to decide for himself, and for him to walk into my office with his own two feet. I was curious, but for him, he must have tossed and turned all night without respite.

But he did respond later that day. "I will try." Our conversation was brief, and his response, even shorter, but he must have worried over this decision for hours. I was thankful. We had communicated fully, man-to-man. As I had hoped, he became an excellent director of Hanil General Hospital.

I must tell you now, dear reader, that Noh passed from this Earth 11 years ago. I respected him enormously, as he was one of our best employees to date. I regret not having been able to return his personal favor to the business and me before he passed; may he rest in peace.

Let us return to the past. The following day, the new post for the chief executive director of the hospital was made public. As for Noh's right hand man, or the chief of operations and business development, I picked Cho Chang-gu. This news was met with some trepidation. The hospital staff and doctors, etc. were shocked. The double threat of Noh's charisma, coupled with Cho's "bulldozer-like" personality, changed the atmosphere of the hospital entirely. This is because the hospital's CEO finally acted like he owned the place, but in a good way; the new "owner" had finally emerged from the ashes.

A month later, I visited Hanil General Hospital. Thanks to the chief of operations and business development's daily reports, I knew the daily comings and goings, so to speak, but I was able to view with my own eyes how much the hospital had changed. First of all, it was cleaner. I found out later that they had renovated the entrance and changed the lighting, to make it brighter. The character of the hospital had also changed. It was full of life and vigor.

Three months passed. The number of occupied hospital beds jumped from less than 40 percent close to full capacity. On every front, numerically speaking, the management index rose. I became full of confidence. My next step: requesting a meeting with the Vice Premier.

"Stop by my office this year, after the operations settlement report is complete."

The Vice Premier, through a mole, had already been receiving reports on how the hospital was doing. That is why from then on, the quarterly reports were changed to yearly reports. What to make of this? It meant that the Vice Premier would judge the hospital's profitability on a yearly basis, rather than on quarterly reports.

The wishes of KEPCO's employees had been granted. The success of the economic policy of state-owned corporations such as ours owes a life's debt to people such as him.

"Thank you!"

CHAPTER 5

Number One in Management Assessment

Hanil General Hospital in Ssangmun-dong

In 1983, the South Korean government implemented the "State-Owned Companies and Their Management Assessment." It evaluated 24 state-owned companies and their management performance over the course of a year. The Korea Electric Power Corporation (KEPCO) placed first in 1983. The prize money of 5 billion KRW, coupled with a year-end bonus for employees, made everyone happy. The monetary prizes and the pride we felt as number one was all in thanks to the South Korean government's economic planning board.

During the past year, we had worked hard, and while we were happy with our grade of "A," my heart was somewhat heavy. There was still a debt that had to be paid. Hanil General Hospital's management was weighing heavily on my mind. The previous year, it had managed to shrink its losses by about a third, but it was falling behind and wasn't turning a profit. I had not been able to keep my promise to the South Korean government, and the Vice Premier had only allowed me to keep soldiering on because of his generosity.

I felt even worse because in truth, it was nearly impossible to make Hanil General Hospital profitable. The chief executive officer of the hospital, Noh Tae-il and his support team had done their very best. Actually, they had worked themselves to exhaustion over the past year without respite (they didn't even take their vacation days), and yet, the end result was shrinking losses by only a third. To turn a profit, it would have to occupy at least 250 hospital beds.

So there are some limits to working hard and doing your best. Sometimes, there is a wall that cannot be scaled by mere human abilities. Did this mean that I would forever be indebted to the Vice Premier (for allowing the hospital to keep running for mostly KEPCO employees)?

I felt stuck. I remembered with trepidation meeting the Vice Premier only a year ago, and I remembered him getting up from his seat, and his fatherly stance. I remembered being drawn to his gentleness and his humanity. He was careful not to talk too much, but I remembered his expression, and now, I could sense something.

Looking back, his expression told me everything I needed to know; in truth, I felt like he had been saying with his face that, "CEO Park, there are some things that are simply not worth it. Your youthful vigor and earnestness will buy you a year, but a year later, I hope you learn a bittersweet lesson." He had already known that it couldn't be done. That I would know of this a year later, I was filled with regret.

They say sometimes it is necessary to change one's thinking. This means that it's a new game, with new rules. I decided to scrap Hanil General Hospital (the one in its original location). This was my reasoning: "No matter how much I try, I cannot break the ceiling. It's better to be swift in my decisions. If I want the hospital to be profitable, then I am going to clear the proverbial chessboard. I am going to build a new hospital. This is the only way forward," I thought to myself.

"Where should we build it? At Ssangmun-dong. We can convert the training institute into a hospital. It is a large building, situated on a large piece of land. If the training institute was converted, then we could fit in at least 500 hospital beds, plus more. With the rest of the land left over, let's build an apartment building. We could cover the cost of building the new hospital with funds from selling the Seosomun-dong hospital," I thought.

After a lot of twists and turns, the new hospital for KEPCO was built at Ssangmun-dong. With the building of this new hospital, the employees of KEPCO had their long-cherished wish granted. With 31 departments in medicine eventually (it started with 24), it would become one of the few general hospitals in northern Seoul at the time, contributing not only to the health of KEPCO employees but also that of nearby residents.

The Apartment Business

During the early 1980's in South Korea, it was not easy for a salaryman to own an apartment unit. For a decent apartment, the price would run to at least 50 million won. That is why one of the greatest wishes of the employees back then was to own an apartment. "Well, since we have addressed the problem with the hospital by relocating it, why don't we use this opportunity to build an apartment for them as well."

I called the director of management and the union head to build a housing cooperative. I laid down a billion won in funds to finance this building, which was derived from most of the prize money that we had won previously from the South Korean government.

We started the construction work right away, and two years later, we had built about 824 apartment units of a small-to-mid-size range. Employees could buy the apartment units outright for about 30 million won. We decided to give those without an apartment of their own first pick.

The apartment business could not have been achieved without the help of KEPCO's union. Our union was sometimes laughed at for being a company-dominated union. However, my opinion stands that our company's union was the model example of how a union should behave. I say this now, like I said before, that our union heads for top-notch. Let me name a few of them here: Jang Hwal-soo, Lee Jong-wan, Choi Tae-il. They were all for a win-win for both the company and for the employees.

It may be hard to believe, but for us, there was no conflict between management and the labor union then. For me, it meant drinking tea several times with the head of the labor union, and after inspections in other provinces, drinking rice wine with everyone. The labor union's purpose should always be to protect the rights of the workers and their benefits. The wish of the chief executive officer should always coincide with this purpose. If we were both aiming towards the same goal, then why would we fight? If they wanted something, we gave them twice of what they wanted.

Sometimes the company could not give them anything, but that was fine too. In the latter case, we would talk heart-to-heart. We all understand this. The problem is the CEO's will. I really mean this. Sometimes one party or the other needed to take a step back, to keep each other in check. But paying it forward, most of the time, would work in the company's favor in the years to come. Happy employees result in happy companies.

So it goes that communication is really key, and the most important trait in a relationship between labor unions and a company. A happy relationship between the two will always advance the company. When both parties talk earnestly, then what reason is there to fight?

While we are on this topic, I would like to say a few more words. For today's economy, one of our biggest hurdles is labor unions. The tyranny of a labor union produces many side effects. If we continue along this path, then our society might face ruination. So how are we to proceed?

These days, everyone criticizes labor or trade unions and their leaders, but with all due respect, we should first direct our gaze inward. From the company's nascence, if the CEO or the owner stays honest, then we would not have this kind of impending sense of doom looming over us; I am referring to the disagreements between labor unions and companies. From the first, how many CEOs or those in a position of power abuse their status to harm their subordinates? I hesitate to say this, but it may be what we like to call the "*gap*" and "*eul*" relationship in Korea. "*Gap*" is the one with the power, and "*eul*" is the subordinate, in this instance.

The problem lies in "*gap*" trying to abuse his power and privileges to make the subordinate miserable. He would rather squeeze all that he can from the "*eul*" for his own personal advantage. So what would "*eul*" look like to the "*gap*?" The former would think, "He is not on our side," and immediately start disliking him. This causes, from the onset, a breach of trust.

Even if it's hard, we must put cooperation and mutual trust into practice. This is the way forward, the way towards even greater achievement. This way, "*gap*" and "eul" both survive. "*Gap*" should treat "*eul*" with great respect, as if it were tradition and the law of the land; as long as this holds, this will come to pass. Do we not have excellent precedents in Japan? The Korea Electric Power Corporation (KEPCO) can do it, and likewise, if it can be done in Japan, then it may be possible to implement this everywhere.

My fellow KEPCO men, with your help, we can build an excellent partnership between management and your labor union!

I would like to encourage management to stay kind. This is the moral mantle of leadership. However, if you are the wiser party, then you should hold your ground. Usually, and I hate to say this, but most labor unions leave destruction in their wake, and the management unfortunately has to repress them. This is why unfortunately you can't be too nice; otherwise they will take advantage of you. The really mean ones are the ones that take advantage of your goodness and start asking for the most impossible rights or conditions and become hoodlums. That is why the management needs to be kind, but firm. We have a Korean saying, which roughly translates to, "The seedling is yellow from the start." This means that it is doomed from the start. Anyone who doesn't abide by the ingrained laws of ethical behavior is doomed from the start. A leader should choose to confront the union. The worst might come, but that's fine. If a leader surrenders to injustice and unreasonable obstinacy, things will get only worse. If your counterpart is out of the spectrum of common sense, it means that they are hopeless. If a leader steps back, it will give a breather for the time being. However, in the long run, a leader will have to give in everything, and he will be robbed of everything. What remains is nothing but insult. It is better to shut down the door. This level of determination is what we need to confront them. How odd. The real winner is the one who concedes first. This is an irony. In Korean, we have a phrase called, "*sajeuk pilsaeng*." It means, "If you're determined to die, you will live." There is sometimes a literal need to end things. That is why personally, I would rather just be bold and fight if I am in the right.

If management allows lawlessness and gives into threats, then everything collapses like a pile of dominoes. It will end in ruin for the company as a whole. That is why the management needs to heed its duty in tending to its flock, and remember the importance of wise leadership.

I spoke too much. These are (just) my thoughts. Please look upon my opinions kindly.

With regards to how the prize money was spent, I would like to reiterate something. In the beginning, the entire sum, or 5 billion KRW, was earmarked for all of the employees. But when we realized that that would amount to only about 150,000 KRW to 160,000 KRW, per person, management decided to use this lump sum in a wiser manner.

So for those who suffered from workplace accidents, to retired employees' pensions, to those without home ownership, plenty of possibilities were floated on how to use the money. Another idea that was floated at this time included a power plant association, or club, and the sticking point: an apartment building for those without their own homes.

This association planned to prepare 500 million won for a fund, and on the other hand, made an arrangement to obtain small-sized project orders from the KEPCO, to make ends meet to get the organization going. The club, however, was rather late in making the foundation, which meant that it was not able to properly function as a friendly club, and it was beyond its capacity to support and manage a large number of members. It took time for the club to settle down, thanks to the leaders like Shin Ki-jo, Seong Nak-jeong, and Lee Jong-hun, who all are highly respected by the KEPCO people.

Since 2012, the association has been going from strength to strength, ever since Choi Ki-jeong, a graduate of Seoul National University's School of Law, was appointed as its chief executive officer. He was like a tiger. He spoke in baritone. He was a man of action, and there was nothing that he couldn't achieve once he set his mind to it. The association saw some of its best days under his leadership.

For employees who had sustained workplace injuries, the initial money that had been earmarked for them, or about 200 million KRW, was supplemented by an additional 1.3 billion KRW. By 1987, the funds grew to 2.2 billion KRW. It grew to cover employees' living expenses, as well as scholarships for their children.

The Kyunghyang Shinmun's Grand Prize in Energy

For any (developed) country, it's important to establish prizes in areas that are important and or need further development. The Republic of Korea has several prizes regarding culture and the arts, and such, but until recent years, there was no prize in the field of energy. No one seems to understand the importance of energy for a country like ours. As soon as I was appointed the CEO of KEPCO, I realized the importance of establishing an "Enertopia," and the need for a prize in this area.

Enertopia is a word that I have created, a portmanteau, combining the nouns, "energy" and "utopia." The Enertopia that I have envisioned is a country that generates over 50 percent of its own power needs, and does much to encourage the use and the support of energy generation and efficiency. It also speaks to innovation in energy.

For South Korea, we simply do not have enough natural resources. That is why an Enertopia is an oasis that is difficult to reach for our country. There are many different types of energy, such as nuclear energy, energy from fossil fuels, to solar power, etc., and yet, it is my belief that we need to increase environmentally friendly ways of generating power. This means more research and innovation is needed in this area. To inject new energy into those who work in this field, I feel like a grand prize is necessary. Who will take the lead? Should this not be the work of KEPCO? This is why *The Kyunghyang Shinmun*'s Grand Prize in Energy was created.

Initially, it was envisioned as a prize covering the entire energy sector, but it was decided that it would be unreasonable for KEPCO to oversee it, so it was targeted only at the electrical energy sector. In any case, the Enertopia I advocate is to secure energy through nuclear power, so I accepted the idea.

We decided to award the prize to individuals and to groups. The grand prize awarded to a group became a Presidential Award (10 million won), followed by the Prime Minister's Awards awarded to four separate groups (3 million won each), and the highest prize for individuals being the Prime Minister's Award (3 million won), followed by the Minister's Award awarded to eight individuals (1 million won). The total prize money as well as the awards ceremony would cost about 50 million KRW. The real problem lay with the department of management. At first, when we envisioned the award, it was supposed to be awarded by KEPCO. However, the general consensus was that a news organization should award the prizes, to ensure that the distribution of the awards would remain honest and fair.

This is why *The Kyunghyang Shinmun*'s Grand Prize in Energy was created. We decided to form a partnership with the newspaper and donated some funds to them. We donated 1 billion KRW in total with the understanding that the awards would continue, long after my tenure. During those times, the amount of money that KEPCO initially donated would accrue interest of up to six or seven percent, generating enough money to cover some of the costs, at least. The initial seed money for this venture came from KEPCO ranking number one in management assessment in 1983. The first presidential energy award was awarded to Pohang Iron and Steel Company, now known as POSCO, in October 1985.

I did some sleuthing recently, and was astounded to hear that those at the same newspaper were unaware of the grand energy prize. Alas, dear reader, I am sorry to tell you that the 24th energy awards ceremony became the last of its kind in this field. This was back in 2008. This is what the world is coming to, may it rest in peace.

Employees' Vacation Resorts

In the early 1980s, employees and their families used to vacation at a remote company facility that was sometimes called the KEPCO Training Center. It had 80 rooms, along with a restaurant, a game room, and an assembly hall. But the real secret was this: hot springs. No other company during those days had access to thermal water. Every year, about 7,000 employees would vacation there and it catered to the well-being of employees. The only problem was that it could not, even at full capacity, house all the employees and their families every year. It was my belief that at least once a year, an employee should take four days off at a company resort. This is why we built a second condominium in Sokcho, Gangwon Province.

KEPCO owned the land, and it was a perfect place to build. In 1987, construction was completed. We didn't know this while we were building the condo, but three years later, we found thermal springs here too. That is why the price of the land increased exponentially. KEPCO is truly blessed.

It was not easy, building the second condominium. Suanbo, Chungju-si, Chungcheongbuk-do, was a well-known place, so most of the land had owners. But as luck would have it, a man who owned 13,223.14 square meters of land across from a church, put his land on the market. The land originally had been a pear orchard. I found out later that the company man we sent to buy the land was instrumental in securing this site for us. While KEPCO was doing well, it was through the hidden efforts of employees like him.

The second training center had a garden nearby, and you could even stroll there. The building itself had 92 individual rooms along with an assembly hall, a gymnasium, and an exhibition hall, and became a training center in name only; it was a truly great place to relax.

CHAPTER 6

Wolseong Espionage Incident

"Jindogae One" Launch

On August 4, 1983, I headed to Jeju Island for a much needed vacation. All my immediate family members came with me. It was my first vacation in about 10 years. Why? After starting my second career as a business executive, I did not take a single day off. All my colleagues did the same; so don't take this the wrong way. Every CEO during those days worked extremely hard.

After checking in at the hotel and unpacking, we all headed to the beach. I loved the sense of freedom it brought me, but I took more pleasure in seeing my family so happy again.

The next day, I woke up early, as I usually do. But alas, I could not help but worry about a particular nuclear reactor site, located in Kori. It seemed to be saying to me, "Please visit me." I felt like it was a message from the heavens.

I rose from my seat. I woke up my secretary, Kim Mun-kyung, who was sleeping in the next room.

Section Chief Kim Mun-kyung. A graduate of Korea University, he had been my personal assistant since my days at Korea Heavy Industry and Construction (KHIC). From the very beginning at our prior workplace, human resources selected him from a pool of candidates with excellent qualifications. When asked why he applied for the company by an interviewer, he explained that President Park, the CEO, seemed "real" to him. What on Earth did he mean by this? I came upon this story later via a colleague of his. Kim explained that he had been in the ROTC and had received a letter from me, inviting him to join the company ranks. He licked his finger, and touched the signature on the letter. It smeared. At this, he was astounded. There must have been at least 8,000 members in the ROTC of which he had been a member. This meant that the CEO must have signed all of them. All 8,000 letters. Imagine that. This made him want to work for me.

I really consider him to be one of my best subordinates to date, because he valued "true" and was always interested in self-development. He had majored in Chinese during university, and he was fluent in English as well as Japanese. This is one of the reasons why I couldn't quite put down a book because I was motivated by watching him always study. He is currently the head of the cooperation department of a power generation company and the future president of the company.

I told him to not contact Jeju Island's branch or the company headquarters, but to book two flights to Busan. For those remaining behind, he was instructed to tell them that I had urgent business to attend to in Seoul. There were no direct flights to Busan, so we got a ticket from Jeju to Gimhae via Gimpo. Upon arrival, I booked a taxi. Since the connecting flights were so complicated, it took a while for me to get my bearings.

When I finally got to the Kori Nuclear Reactor site, I asked the front desk to see the power plant manager. The head of the division branch of

Kori was vacant because Min Kyung-sik, who had been the director of the department until recently, was transferred to the head of the management department at the headquarters in Seoul.

The security guard asked me who I was and what brought me to his place of employment that day. At this, my loyal secretary bristled and said that I was the CEO of KEPCO. The security guard was rude, and stared at me. The CEO of the company that he worked for had shown up in a shabby taxi. Traditionally, if the CEO wanted to schedule a meeting with the division head, then it usually took a month of finely-tuned, precise preparation. I had caught him (and them) unawares.

The security guard was skeptical, but placed a phone call to company headquarters. It was a very long phone call. The security guard's voice started getting louder and louder. The company headquarters did not seem to understand the situation either.

After what seemed like eons, a man came running from the office. The office was situated some distance from the reactor site. At the sight of me, standing like I was lost in thought, my subordinate started running even faster. His face had gone ashen-faced. Upon reaching where I was, I could not help but notice his big, round eyes. He saluted me. He must have been flustered. He couldn't speak. After catching his breath, he said, "President Park, what brings you to us?"

He blurted the words out. The even more astonished security guard also saluted me. I fist bumped my subordinate's shoulder and said, "Go."

I spoke quietly, without a steely-edge to my voice. It was not in my nature for all sorts of fuss to be made just because I had made a surprise appearance, and I felt sorry.

"To where, sir?"

"Your office, of course."

The employee still looked befuddled and entered the security guard's quarters and held a phone to his ear as he prepared to dial someone for more instructions.

"Here, there's no need for you to make a phone call." I didn't even wait for his response. I started my way down the long corridor. He exited the security guard's quarters and started sprinting towards me. Kim and the security guard followed.

"Please, take good care of President Park!"

The employee shouted this whilst running in the other direction. For him, it was more important to let his own boss know that I was here, rather than escorting me himself.

As soon as I neared the reactor, another employee ran out. He issued a somewhat rushed greeting, then welcomed me to his office. He was the manager of the nuclear power plant. Everyone must have gone home. Unbeknownst to everyone, a lot of time had passed.

"Should I put the kettle on for some tea?" He was still startled.

I could almost hear his thoughts in my head; "Why is he here? At this hour? To Kori, a far-flung place from Seoul? Without making an earlier appointment?"

It appeared as though he could not process what was going on in his head.

"The tea can wait. Come over and sit by me."

He carefully sat, at some distance from me.

"Listen to me. Please deploy your five-minute standby unit (normally smaller than the size of a 30-men platoon) immediately."

His face went pale from shock. After some initial hesitation, he ran outside.

I waited and waited. And waited some more. I think an hour must have passed. With no flight squadron deployed, instead, another power plant manager appeared.

"President Park, what brings you here?" It was the chief of the department, Choi Jang-dong. He was and remains a man I respect highly today, an elite of the elites, or so they say in Korean.

Trailing him closely was the reserve company commander, and many top-level officials. As soon as they had received word of an alarm, they had raced over 30 km over to this place, from Busan's Haeundae beach area, where they had probably been resting at their company quarters. In seconds, the office was filled with people. The tension in the air seemed to evaporate, and a congenial atmosphere replaced it somewhat, although we were still on edge.

The reserve company commander stepped out for a second then returned and said that five-minute standby unit was ready to move. It was over an hour and a half since the alarm had first been raised. He lowered his head with shame. It was probably the first time that the five-minute standby unit was called to assemble. They were in fact not ready because they had not been practicing their drills properly.

While this was going on, another person on duty ran in. He whispered something to the power plant manager.

With fear in his voice, the power plant manager said, "President Park, I have word that the Jindogae One alert has been issued."

"What do you mean? This is a drill that I have ordered, but it's not a real situation."

"Yes, I am aware of that, sir. But a real Jindogae One alert has been issued. There is word that North Korean spies have infiltrated Wolseong."

"What?" Now I was on edge.

"Then give me a full report immediately!"

In his report, about 5 km from our Wolseong Nuclear Power Plant, South Korean Marines had captured a North Korean ship. After a round of firing between the two, four spies had been killed. The spy ship had also sunk. This was the work of the 7th Regiment of the South Korean Marine. Thanks to them, the drill had turned into a real one.

There were some voices of discontent over me having issued an emergency drill. As a company, it was hard enough as is, to deal with everyday operations. This was true. But I disagree. Daily management is a basic necessity and a must. But there are other dangers lurking nearby that can make a company face ruin: wars, natural disasters, terrorism, etc. While I was at the Korea Heavy Industry and serving as the CEO, my first emergency call was to the factory fire brigade. If a fire had destroyed everything, then regardless of whether we were conducting our day-to-day operations well, the company would have gone bust.

The Korea Electric Power Corporation (KEPCO) was a different type of beast, as we were also what South Korea dubs a "National Information Infrastructure." If one of our electricity generators stopped working, for example, some of the country would have become paralyzed. If one of our nuclear reactors burst, then our country would have had to deal with a national disaster. Natural disasters could also happen, and likewise, we are still technically at war with the North. A CEO who is careless with regards to safeguarding national security is derelict in one of his foremost duties, in my opinion.

Chinese Civilian Aircraft Flies over Restricted Air Space

A few months prior: "Fellow citizens, this is not a drill."

On May 5, 1983, around 2 p.m., there was an urgent news alert issued by a public broadcaster, the Korea Broadcasting System (KBS). This sparse yet serious alert made everyone jittery and on edge. It was soon revealed that a Chinese civilian aircraft had accidently flown into restricted airspace and had to "make an emergency landing" at Chuncheon. A U.S. Army base was located there. Everyone seemed to breathe a sigh of relief that this had been cause of the urgent news alert.

Coincidentally, I was at a branch of KEPCO, north of Seoul, for an unscheduled inspection. I wanted to catch my employees unawares at the Uijeongbu branch, and that's where I was when I heard the news. I was near the border between the two Koreas. When the distressed employees found out that the president of the company was at their headquarters (they had been told by a very flustered security team), they hurriedly came to the entrance and bowed. The head of the branch, Bae Kyung-joo, and his close aides were all assembled within seconds. Instead of being pleased, he was probably surprised and caught off guard myself.

"Please, this way, President Park."

"Branch manager, please place your squad on a five-minute standby!"

"I am sorry. But I, as the president of the company, am here to put your employees on alert." I thought.

I spoke a bit coldly but I closed my eyes to contain my frustration, then issued the order myself. At first, my direct subordinate seemed flustered. Then he went into action by calling the reserve forces' company commander and the chief of general affairs. I had caused a little bit of a commotion. About 10 minutes later, the squad was standing by the entrance. But panic had set in because it had coincided with the alert from KBS. It was too close for comfort, to dismiss it as mere coincidence. It was like it had been preordained. That evening, I dined with the bosses of the power plant located in Uijeongbu. We ate noodles in cold beef broth, called "*naengmyun*," in Korean.

I dined with Choi Sei-chang, the Minister of National Defense a few days later.

"CEO Park, who is in charge of intelligence at KEPCO?"

"The Planning and Management Office." I spoke informally.

"CEO Park, if you try to hold another unannounced alert, please notify me first."

KEPCO became super busy again. We would have to report to the Minister of Defense too, from now on. This would become a blessing and a curse in disguise.

CHAPTER 7

Cultivating Talent

Gongneung-dong Training Institute

"Nobody is more professional than I am!" This is the motto of the U.S. Army Corps of Noncoms. How full of pride is this motto? The sense of pride that they take in their work is because they believe that they are the best of the best. This is how noncoms in the U.S. Army feel, and in truth, they really are one of a kind. That is why the U.S. Army is strong.

It is my personal belief that this is due to training and hard work. A man is not born, but rather, he is made. A talented man must be cultivated. Most U.S. soldiers have not gone to college (compared with 60 percent of Korean soldiers who have completed higher education). If they do go to college, they do so by earning a scholarship during their service. Sometimes they are not even high school graduates. With these resources, the United States makes the world's strongest army. This is the result of education (during their stint in the army) and assiduousness.

During my tenure at the Korea Electric Power Corporation (KEPCO), there was an area that I devoted some time to, and this was "*Injae yangseong*," or the cultivation of talent. If someone wants to help someone else grow, I believed that a top-class training institute would do the trick. That is why from our pool of qualified employees, we analyzed their work output and temperaments then trained all of them, from the highest to the lowest, the latter of which generally worked in technical divisions. This meant that we would need at least four to five training institutes and or research centers. If these were scattered across the nation, it would create more problems in terms of management and upkeep. That is why my original idea was to have them located closely, in one area.

One of the best out of possible sites back then was a place in Ansan, near the Banwol Industrial Complex. It was a hilly area of about 660,000 meters squared. I remember that the then executive director Yun Hee-woo, showed me around this site when I was first appointed to head KEPCO. But an even better site turned out to be located in today's Gong-neung-dong. The first of South Korea's Institute of Atomic Energy Research was built in Gongneung-dong. In 1959, the historic first nuclear reactor for our country was installed there, the TRIGA Mark-2 (100KW). In 1997, unfortunately, this reactor was dismantled and turned into a cultural treasure site.

Like I said before, the location near Bulamsan Mountain seemed to be the best place. It had the most beautiful scenery of mountains and green areas. It already had about 26,000 square meters where buildings were situated, with about 720,000 square areas of land left over. Accounting for building costs, it was much less expensive than Ansan. I decided to buy it for the company. It was my thinking that it would become the best training institute near Seoul. I also thought it may become one of the best in Asia. I bought this treasure for 13.7 million U.S. dollars.

It opened in September 1986, and was dubbed KEPCO Central Training Center. At the time, the chief of the department was Lee Chang-sup, a man who had graduated from Kyunggi High School and Seoul National University. Lee was a veteran in the field of power distribution, and was a man of learning as well as a man of repute.

The remodeling and opening of the training center was largely thanks to him. The next year, he would be promoted, and serve an even greater role in the success of the company as a whole.

As I have said before, a man is made, not born. This comes from learning. A person learns after many hours of practice, then becomes familiar with it after many months, then after the passage of even more time, becomes comfortable, then finally, becomes an expert.

The strongest army in the entire world, the U.S. Army, is notable for its advancement of learning; this is what sets it apart from others. For soldiers as well as noncommissioned officers, to officers, they have to undergo training for at least two years. After being commissioned, junior-level officers take OBC (Officer Basic Course) and OAC (Officer Advanced Course) courses, and field-level officers take strategic-level education at Army, Navy, and Air Force Colleges, respectively. In case of Army, some are sent to the U.S. Army Command and General Staff College (CGSC). Even after all this training, there is the training of professional personnel, and this results in superior expertise. I would like to name some of the specialized training units in the U.S. Army: Green Berets, Rangers, and Pathfinders. Add Navy Seals, and the Air Force, and many others, too numerous to be mentioned one by one.

This is not all. The United States is always engaged in warfare. After the American Revolution, there has not been a single day of rest for the U.S.

Army, metaphorically speaking, of course. These include: the American Indian Wars, the American Civil War, the Spanish-American War, World War I and World War II, the Korean War, the Vietnam War, the Iraq War, and the war in Afghanistan. Through continuous fighting, in theory as well as practice, has made them invincible.

An organization or nation must teach and nurture those with talent, then through practice, turn them into experts. This will birth a powerful company, and a powerful country.

I aspired to make KEPCO a strong company by following similar guidelines. Through a series of training for all personnel and new employees, I strove to make experts out of them all. This is when the mid-to long-term personnel talent program came to be. For the best of the best, we sent them to Harvard University, the Massachusetts Institute of Technology, the University of Tokyo, and created financial resources and secured paths for them to go to top universities. About 200 employees were picked to undergo job training at other companies, for hands-on-job apprenticeships. Some were sent to training institutes within the country. After this initial first program ended, 10 years later, the plan was for there to be 150 employees with Ph.D.'s, 400 employees with master's degrees, and so on; in other words, create a company of talented men.

Around this time, we also picked employees from the first- and second-class to undergo management courses. A top-notch mind was important, but so was practical knowledge and experience in business operations. All these people would become the driving force of the organization. Because we were trying to cut costs, the training period for these employees was about six months, but the graduates of the program would come to boast skills that we hoped were comparable to those with MBA's from the world's best universities.

The number of employees that received training in country were about 40 in number every year. We donated money to Seoul National University, and everyone who graduated from the six-month program earned a certificate of completion from the university's Graduate School of Business. This process served as a talent pool and helped the human resources department in the management of executive-level personnel.

Kori Nuclear Power Plant Training Center

In mid-1984, the director of the Nuclear Power Construction submitted a document. The document requested that the byproducts from the former Kori warehouse site be returned to its original state and the site returned to the local provincial government.

The director's name was Shim Chang-saeng, and he was the top nuclear energy specialist at KEPCO. In later years, he would be responsible for the installation of nuclear reactors Younggwang 3 and 4, and would also design the first South Korean APR1400, a more advanced type of a nuclear power plant.

I called him, "Enertopia." He was the one I thought would fulfill my dreams of having South Korea become a utopia of energy generation and efficiency. And he did, for he became an expert in the field of nuclear energy and would even make contact with the United Arab Emirates (UAE) and export South Korean nuclear reactors to the aforementioned country in the future.

The land where was 80,000 square kilometers of agricultural land we had been storing materials for the past 15 years to build reactors of Kori 1 and 2. It had been a kind of dumping ground for this type of waste for about 15 years. Land near power plants is a precious commodity that will one day be useful to us. It is difficult to buy land near nuclear power plants, but even harder to manage them. I thought to myself that we couldn't let such a treasure go. I told my subordinates to buy the land immediately. The next day, we were told that purchasing the land would be difficult. This was because even if we owned it, it was part of a "green belt." A "green belt" dated back to President Park Chung-hee's administration, where some land was to be protected from reckless development. The program was designed for the conservation of some land. If it was part of the "green belt," then there really was a problem. The removal of this status would be up to the president of the country.

"CEO Park, give up. The answer is no!"

"But we are trying to save a barren land."

"Even the president authorized just *one* of the 'green belts' status be removed."

It looked impossible. But I couldn't resist. If I wanted South Korea to become an Enertopia, then I needed the land to build another training center, and it needed to be near a nuclear reactor site, near Kori. And wasn't this land so close to where the nuclear reactors were? How could we just let go of such a good opportunity?

I had some business matters to attend to in Kori anyway, so I went there myself. It was a piece of land that I really wanted to buy for the company. Upon my return to the company headquarters, I asked Shim to take some photos showing the "bad" condition of the land, and prepare an aerial view of a potential training center that would be built there.

After a few days, I prepared a chart. It had one photo of the current conditions of the land, another photo of an aerial view of a training center, along with the need for a training center; in short, three short "slides."

I asked them to arrange a meeting. After several days, I heard back from them. A senior economics officer arranged the meeting between the South Korean President and me.

"What brings you here today?"

I opened my chart.

"This is for the dissolution of the 'green belt' [located in Kori]. Mr. President!"

"The 'green belt'? That's a no." With one word, he refused.

I almost blacked out. With my head lowered, I waited. And waited some more.

"There are only three 'slides' to this presentation. Please just let me continue."

For me, this was like a life or death situation. If I missed this golden opportunity, then it would all be over. When a person works to his hardest, then God intervenes, or so they say. For a while, the room was silent. For me, it seemed like eternity.

"Ok, fine. Let's see it."

I first opened the first "slide," which showed a hilly "wasteland." This I followed with a beautifully constructed piece of architecture, which had the blueprint of what the proposed building would look like. This was a drastic change. It was so beautiful that anyone would be swayed to our view. Then I opened the last "slide." With all my soul, I poured forth my explanation. It was a short one. I am sure that my voice was shaking by this point.

A long silence followed. It must have been brief, but to me, it felt long. But to me, like I said before, it felt like an eternity. My head was still lowered, and I breathed in and out. A silence as deep as an abyss followed.

"Fine. Bring me the documents."

This is how the current KHNP Human Resource Development Center came to be. As of this writing, the KEPCO International Nuclear Graduate School (KINGS) is also located there. There are about 55 students from abroad from 19 different countries, and the student body is about 120 in number. It has become a place for experts in nuclear technology to conduct research.

Electric Power Research Institute in Daedeok

In the summer of 1984, I was visiting France's Electricite de France S.A. (EDF). During the middle of a discussion, the EDF Chairman and CEO said to me, "Monsieur Park, we are about to stage a competition with primary energy sources."

What was this? I doubted my own ears. Competing with gas or oil using at home? Was this not the dream of electricity companies such as us? As fine and forward thinking as France was, to replace gas and oil with electricity! It came as a shock to me. But it was straight from his mouth, so I could only but believe.

When I returned to South Korea, I consulted a few key people, and found that the Chairman and CEO of EDF was right to be a bit boastful about its new blue ocean. At the company, there were already at least 300 employees with Ph.D.'s, and the EDF would take care of France's energy supply plans. The nuclear energy also provided over 60 percent of the country's total power supply (over 80 percent now) and even exported electricity to neighboring countries; to me, this felt like an unachievable dream.

"That's right. If EDF could, then how could we, KEPCO, not?" A sense of pride that I do not want to lose intrigued me.

This ended up as a daydream, but when I was first appointed at KEPCO as the CEO, I dreamt of establishing an academic institution worthy of being the Korean version of the United States' Massachusetts Institute of Technology. However, Fate had other plans. The high school affiliated with KEPCO, Soodo Industry High School, was still important to me, but in order to lead in a new world order and be competitive in it, I needed to recruit the best and the brightest for a higher institution of learning. But after a while, I quietly gave up on this dream. There were too many hurdles, and far too many mountains to overcome. So instead, I decided to establish a training institute/laboratory to mold the minds of the truly gifted brains. The reason why I pushed forward with this effort, as with the Gongneung-dong Training Center, was because of this second wish of mine. I thought to myself that one day, in a better environment, the training center that I mentioned previously would someday house a wing with the finest minds of Korea.

But the problem behind the laboratory was that the Ministry of Science and Technology and I squabbled over where it should be established. The HR said that it was right to place it in Daedeok. Daedeok was already a place where the greatest minds congregated. And, for the foreseeable future, it would be one of the places for our country's research hub. As such, they advised me to cooperate with the nearby research laboratories.

Daedeok was Daedeok, but Seoul was still Seoul. I decided to leave the Gongneung-dong Training Institute as it was, and strive to make it better, while at the same time, figure out what to do with Daedeok. But what luck. A second research complex was being built, so I decided to purchase 120,000 *pyeong*, or about 4.26 million square feet of land that it would stand on. The land it was situated on lay at the foot of Hwabong Mountain (200 m). Among South Korea's laboratories, the surrounding land and the vista it provides may move some to tears, even today. Not only this, but the land itself is very accessible by car. What do I mean by this? To the south is a tunnel. It is called Daedeok Tunnel. At the onset, the construction of the tunnel was somewhat delayed because the people who lived near it always called it a useless piece of land, not fit for anything. That is why we were able to pick the land of our choosing. The work progressed quickly, because of the quick-witted vice president of KEPCO, Yun Hee-woo.

Securing (and Retaining) Talent

I had, by now, achieved two things in order to secure and retain talent: established the Gongneung-dong Training Institute and bought land where Daedeok's laboratory would stand. But the real heart of the matter lies with the people, and not the company. In order to catch up to the likes of EDF, we needed to commit ourselves to doing many things.

The first order of business was to secure excellent human resources. Education, training, would be more affordable, and after undergoing these two prerequisites, I believed the production numbers would rise.

Soon after I was appointed the CEO, I met with a professor from a certain university and met some of his soon-to-graduate students. During our discussion, what surprised me was that KEPCO was not popular at all. To me, it came as a shock. One of them even said to me, "Is [your] company a place for [elites] like us?"

I glared back and forth between the student and the professor, and then gathered my bearings. The group, now somewhat embarrassed, explained to me that KEPCO was viewed as a tax collector, literally collecting electricity bills and climbing up and down the electric poles as KEPCO pleased.

I thought to myself then, “How dare these people look at us this way and judge us like this,” and felt a sense of grief mingled with a righteous rage. But I hid this behind an easy laugh and smile, and then patiently explained KEPCO’s current business operations. As for me, I needed their understanding, and that is because the company needed them, people like them, gifted and smart, for the foreseeable future. The problem was our laziness, so the fault indeed (as I did not wish to admit this probably at the time) lay with us. It was not their fault.

The very next day, I called the head of the management division, Min Kyung-sik, to my office. He had headed the nuclear division of the Kori Nuclear Power Plant until recently. Even though his recent reassignment seemed out of place, there was a reason I assigned him to this administrative, managerial position. I explained the dreadful atmosphere of the prior day’s college visit, and discussed ways to resolve the issue. The mutual conclusion that we reached was that we would have to do the publicity campaign ourselves. Then he said that he would personally visit the universities himself from now on.

For a few months, Min and his team went on a university tour of sorts. He was an excellent public speaker and presenter, and since vice president Min had taken this job upon himself, the results spoke for themselves. I would realize later that the magazine that was popular between recent graduate job-seekers, then named “Recruit,” would report that KEPCO was a company worth dreaming of. We had beat Hyundai and Samsung, for so long our rivals and foes, in popularity for a while at least. There we stood, tall and proud, ranked number one.

Since KEPCO then became popular amongst the best and the brightest of Korea, we just had to educate (and train) them well. The training institute and academia played well together, so there were no problems there, but the laboratory and research institute was a different kind of ball game.

From the onset, it was an uphill battle. The problem was that they were monolingual. At the Gongneung-dong Training Institute, we increased the amount that we invested, both time and money, but it was of no use. Even after I left the company, I bet you that the fancy education they received abroad was of no use either.

It is useless to build a training and or research institute without securing talent first, and to do this, a person must develop a research and development sector that will astonish the world. But there was a person who resolved these issues brilliantly later on. Let me talk a while about the 11th President and Chief Operating Officer Lee Jong-hun. He is a brilliant businessman, and is unmatched in leadership skills. He was the second case of an internal promotion to the top and was the best of the best in terms of knowledge of nuclear power as well as an excellent CEO.

He started out by reforming the research institute, knowing that the best brains would not be satisfied by its current offerings. He used the worldwide, famous consulting company, McKinsey, to help reform our place.

The head of the research institute was Dr. Kim Han-joong. He was a graduate of Seoul National University's engineering school, and had worked for GTE, now a part of Verizon. For the researchers, Lee decided to pay them extremely well. With the promise of high salaries, KEPCO was able to secure about 100 geniuses that had studied abroad. Being a KEPCO organization, maintaining a different wage system from the headquarters, autonomous management, and having authority over human resources are things that are easier said than done and cannot be dreamed of by public companies. An average person could not have achieved this.

In a few months, the Korea Electric Power Institute would come to be known as the "place where the lights are first switched on in the morning, and the last place where the lights are switched off at Daedeok Science Complex." We were sure, back then, that we would soon come to belong amongst the ranks of the distinguished elite as a world-class electric power company.

This was back in the early 1990s, and the person who helped my successor CEO achieve this feat was none other than the executive director Lee Bong-rae. He had blocked KEPCO's splintering into different divisions with his very body, or so it seemed at the time.

When I think back upon this time, CEO Lee Jong-hun is among one of my most treasured successors at the Korea Electric Power Corporation. He was the very person who had first started the long march for technological independence under my leadership. During my tenure as the president of the KAAF, he served as the senior vice president and in the 1992 and 1996 Olympics, helped the Korean athletes achieve a great victory in the marathon events.

Soon after my appointment, we traveled to Taiwan together for business purposes. I realized the value of his insight and upright character then, and believed that for the company to grow in the future, he would come to play an instrumental role. Before he was appointed a vice-president, he had served in various posts at the Kori Nuclear Power Plant. I had personally cleared the background check for his appointment.

He came to mean much more to me than just a fellow colleague; he feels more like a brother, even now. Even in his eighties, he still works with me for promotional events for the advancement of Korean athletics. To date, he has shared with me great joys, and well as great sorrows. He is a source of great happiness for me, or what we call "*hongbok*," in Korean.

In life, there are sure to be ups as well as downs. Our luck changed. In 1998, the research institute would hit a wall. Not only this, but KEPCO was fissured into different divisions, a demerger. We may be all bound to history's (sometimes) cruel twists of fate, but I have yet to see a person who can turn back the wheels of time.

Alas! When will KEPCO's time of liberation come to pass?

But I say unto you now, our KEPCO brethren, the way forward is where God's will lies. Like they say in the Western world, when there's a will, there's a way.

No matter what the task is, you must jump in with an iron will. If we want to reclaim the old glory of KEPCO gone by, we must unite for a better tomorrow that has been promised to us.

During the time before Christ, the Jewish people were scattered to the ends of the Earth. But look at them now! 2,000 some years later, did they not gather to establish the country of Israel?

Try, try, and try even harder. Our KEPCO men! Now, we may be scattered about, but our home is really KEPCO. Let us all work together to reclaim the glory days of our company.

Sponsoring Youth Football Teams

What was the most extraordinary among KEPCO's projects to nurture future talents could be found in our support of the youth football team. This project aimed to select 50 elementary schools around the country, and support them. Every year, we selected four to five schools in nine provinces, big cities excluded, and gave a financial support of 10 million won each. For the company, this cost us a cool 500 million South Korean won every year, but it was worth every won, in my humble opinion. As a state-owned, public company, it was a type of social contribution, a type of giving back to the community at large. But moreover, it forged a close association with the community and Korea as a whole. This move would also elevate South Korea's status globally, or so I hoped, for the foreseeable future. But alas, much to my dismay, this all grinded to a halt with the appointment of a certain CEO who shall go unmentioned by name.

In 2014, South Korea failed to advance after the qualifiers for the World Cup. The nation's fans were dismayed. If we chose not to stop this project and continued, I believe that it must have led to a birth of quite a few number of talented, world-renowned players. We would not have been eliminated so early on. Who knows? We may have made the semi-finals, or even the finals. How exciting would that have been?

On July 16, 2014, *The Chosun Ilbo* included a sidebar in one of its articles that is worth noting, even today. During the last World Cup held in Brazil (as of this writing), the article mentions that in Group H, another country that had not seen much play during the past 12 years, managed to win over South Korea. This country was Belgium.

Belgium made it to the quarterfinals, surprising pundits who had predicted otherwise, and ended its winning streak there. Guess what. They had copied us. One of Belgium's power companies, ING Belgium, had sponsored youth football. I digress.

Anyway, in 2000, one of the host countries for the European Cup, Belgium was unable to advance beyond the group matches. To avoid a humiliating defeat, the country started spending money to sponsor young football teams. The national coach, Michel Sablon, spent 10 years coaching young boys from age 7 to age 12. There was science to back the training.

It took 10 years for Belgium to nurture a powerful team that deserves a dream of a championship, but we just wasted 30 years. This makes me give a deep sigh of regret even to this day.

CHAPTER 8

The Ninth Famous Spot in Eastern Korea

Gwandong Gukyung, the Gangneung Branch of KEPCO

In 1984, I visited the Gangneung branch of the Korea Electric Power Corporation. It was to show support for the branch manager, Cho Chang-gu. He was one of the office managers who helped Noh Tae-il, the general director of the former Hanil General Hospital, as we knew it before it was sold. After a tour of the area, we gathered in the branch manager's office for a cuppa.

"President Park, I have a suggestion." He throws this question at me unexpectedly.

"What kind?"

"Can you please rebuild the headquarters in Gangneung?"

This caught me by surprise. How preposterous.

"But why? There is nothing wrong with the one already there."

I knew that he was a fellow who was somewhat strange, but this really took the cake. But then again, fully aware of this character flaw, I had appointed him previously to balance the books at Hanil General Hospital.

I looked at him through narrowed eyes, but a smile escapes my lips. He keeps talking.

"You see, sir…"

He starts talking very quickly. "A branch headquarters is like the provincial seat of the government, and in Gangwon Province, besides Chuncheon, there is one in Gangneung, and Gwandong people are uppity, and…" He drones on and on.

But there is some element of truth to his woeful tale. The current building was dilapidated, from his point of view, and by the train tracks, the neighborhood was bad, and did not live up to KEPCO standards. But it's an absurd suggestion. And how dare he ask me, the CEO of the company, such a thing. But I did not dislike him, for in order to work, we need people like this sometimes.

I needed some time to think. I could have cut him off, but when thinking of how he pulled off the headache-inducing Hanil General Hospital feat (balancing the ledger), I wished to help him.

"Stop talking such nonsense and let's go get some dinner." I stood up.

As we dined together, I thought and thought and thought, and thought some more. "Well, yes, in terms of Gwandong, there is a national treasure there, which is one of the eight famous spots in Eastern Korea (*Gwandong palkyung*). So you think you are great at what you do. Then show me what you can." I thought to myself.

"Fine. If Gwandong is really as great as you say, then a new building there may become another national treasure of Korea."

"Moreover, let's make it to complement the *Gwandong palkyung*. Let's make it another place worth sightseeing. My only condition is that the finished new building meets these criteria."

Cho is quiet for a moment, and stares at me. He looks a bit confused.

"I want us to build a new building that is just as good as the others."

"Does this mean that you approve?" It appears as though he is seeking approval.

"Yes, of course."

Two months passed. From Cho, I received a request for a meeting.

I thought to myself, "Well, he is coming here to see me, but why such urgency for a 'special meeting'?" The following day after I approved this, he entered my office with a large chart.

"Dear President Park, I have found a good place." On the chart, there was a pine grove that looked pretty good.

"So you are saying that the site you discovered is a real deal, good enough to be the ninth famous spot in the area?"

"Just get ready to pay the price, sir. The site is 5000 *pyeong* (177,915 square feet) and it has a great view of the East Sea."

And so it went that this new foray started. So now the burden lay on my side of the bargain. Since the ball was now in my court, I felt that everything was then my responsibility. From the South Korean government, how was I going to receive the funding, which would cost a pretty penny? Also, how to pick the architect or architects who could do this project justice?

I searched high and low for the right person. The one I ended up picking was a new professor from Seoul National University. He had a degree in modern architecture from the Massachusetts Institute of Technology (MIT). Rumor had it that his new research interest was traditional Korean architecture. When I described the project to him, he requested an eight month to one-year term to complete it. I told him, the faster the better.

About eight months later, Professor Kim Jin-gyun brings over the results from the project. He also brings along a bulky blueprint. All in all, it's fabulous. I'm met with a pleasant surprise.

But a worry kept on nagging me. It's supposed to be a KEPCO office building, and yet it will look like a traditional Korean house. But who will have the acuity to understand this and accept it? Even I was caught by surprise. Would the rest of the company accept it? Not only this, but what about the authorities concerned and the business world as a whole?

It was not a project to be rushed. I realized that the first step was to seek approval from within the company. I called Professor Kim to my office again.

"Professor Kim, can you prepare a two-hour presentation of the new building?"

"What do you mean? Like a lecture?"

"Trust me, there's a reason why I want you to do this. I will give you about a month to prep."

We came to a fruitful conclusion. We decided the lecture would take place a month afterwards, during a weekly meeting for executives of the company.

The lecture, as it turned out, was as brilliant as the professor himself. It started with a comparison between Western architecture and East Asian architecture. Then it was followed by the beauty of our traditional Korean architecture, and its many merits. Pre-existing, real world examples were then shown. Well, well, I thought to myself. At the very least we have won over KEPCO's executives, instilling in them a newfound appreciation for traditional *hanok* buildings.

After a week, during another high-level meeting amongst executives,

Professor Kim gave another lecture. This time, it was at the Gangneung branch of the Korea Electric Power Corporation. The pressure was on to create widespread approval for a new sightseeing place that would also be home to the new company headquarters there.

After a week, Professor Kim gave another lecture. This time, it was about the Gangneung branch of KEPCO, *Gwandong gukyung* (Gwandong Ninth). There were people who were surprised, who were praising the work right away, as well as those who were not swayed one bit. Thankfully, the opposition was only around 20 percent.

"Ok, go!" I green-lighted the project.

This is how our newly beloved Gangneung branch was built.

So retrospectively, how did this newly built Gangneung branch live up to its name of becoming the "ninth" sightseeing place of Eastern Korea? For those who came after us, I will try to explain, in layman's terms, some of its merits. Then I must first begin with the *Gwandong palkyung*.

The "*Gwandong palkyung*" refers to the eight sightseeing sights in Eastern Korea. They are located in Gangwon Province, in places that overlook the East Sea. From the North, the first is:

1. Chongseokjeong Pavilion with Haegumgang River's strangely and fantastically-shaped rocks
2. Lake Samilpo in Goseong, where the gods were rumored to stay for three days rather than the planned one day, because the scenery was so beautiful
3. Cheongganjeong Pavilion in Ganseong, which boasts the most beautiful sunrise and sunset over the East Sea. This pavilion was built during the reign of King Jeongjong of the Joseon Dynasty, around

1520 A.D.

4. Naksansa Temple in Yangyang. It was built during the reign of King Munmu of the Shilla Dynasty and is known as one of South Korea's top three "holy sites"
5. Gyeongpodae Pavilion, located north of Gyeongpoho Lake in Gangneung. It is famous for its beautiful vista of the sky, lake, and sea. It is said that the area is also fine for drinking, and one could see the reflection of drinking glasses in the eyes of a loved one.
6. Jukseoru Pavilion in Samcheok. A writer named Jeong Cheol, wrote the "Gwandong Byeolgok," also known as the "Song of Gwandong" while residing here
7. Mangyangjeong Pavilion in Uljin, built during the reign of King Seongjong, around 1690 A.D.
8. Wolsongjeong Pavilion, a place where the Shilla Hwarang, or theatrical performers, enjoyed the beautiful moonlight

So then, how would this Gangneung headquarters office be the ninth famous spot of the region, the *Gwandong gukyung*, so to speak? Let me explain. First, the Gangneung office offers nine kind of virtues. The first virtue comes from the spacious size. The total floor space of the Gangneung headquarters is about 2,500 *pyeong*, and it is big enough to generously support the *Gwandong palkyung*. So the headquarters office is the youngest to be added to the *Gwandong palkyung*, but it is big enough to support the eight older brothers, which are less than 100 to 200 *pyeong* each. The second virtue can be found in the architectural style of the Gwangyeongru, a pavilion designed after the Naksansa Temple and the Changsingak, designed after the Cheongganjeong pavilion. These two pavilions face each other while being the foundation for the KEPCO Gangneung headquarters. This is like a castle built on a solid rock. For the third virtue, let me discuss the Myeongryedang, an auditorium whose solemn name made up of Chinese characters meaning "bright" and "manners," was designed after the Suwon Castle. The fourth virtue can be found in the annex to the west, as it is full of light, remaining true to its name, Deungyeongsa. This very annex was designed after the Seongyojang's guesthouse. The fifth virtue lies in the two big gates of the headquarters office. The left gate is named Gilsangmun, whose Chinese characters mean Good Fortune. The right gate is named Myeonguimun, meaning the Gate of Justice. Both these gates were designed after time-honored guest houses of Gangneung city. The sixth virtue is found in the pond in the center, named Wolyeongji, whose name bears our wish that it would reflect the "glass of Gyeongpo," whose shape is quite in style though it may be young in age. The seventh virtue lies in the fact that the headquarters office site sits modestly in the inland area, while the other eight sites all reign over the ocean or rivers. The eight virtue is found in the name of the central pavilion, which is Gwangyeongru, with a wish that it may sit in the inland area but hopes to be closer at sea at heart. The ninth virtue is discovered in the young spirit of the site, as it is young and strong enough support the eight spots like older brothers. The KEPCO adds another famous spot, and here is the birth of the *Gwandong gukyung*. How glamorous this is.

CHAPTER 9

Settle Your Debts

"I'm Still Alive and Kicking."

On November 25, 1984, Wolseong's Heavy Water Reactor, Unit 1, started leaking. What does this mean? For starters, you have to understand that at KEPCO, we used pressurized heavy water reactors (which makes up about 11 percent of total nuclear reactors that are water-cooled, as of 2022). In these cases, nuclear power creates electricity through pressure and a steam generator, according to the World Nuclear Association. This allows the nuclear reactor to use uranium as fuel. The heat generated from these reactors is then cooled with water.

Heavy Water Reactors, such as the one found in Wolseong, combine water, H_2O, with one element of hydrogen, turning it into D_2O. It is a special type of water that is used to "cool and control nuclear reactions." There are two other types of water-cooled nuclear reactors, which are found more commonly throughout the world and use regular water.

It's a scary thing to have a coolant leak at any reactor, let alone a nuclear one. I am thinking back upon a more recent nuclear disaster that occurred at the Fukushima Daiichi power plant in 2011. The disruption to the power supply and the cooling of three reactors occurred as a result of an earthquake and powerful tsunami near Japan.

Let us return to the Wolseong incident. An emergency alert was issued. The nuclear reactor's temperature was steadily rising. We ascertained that the trouble lay with the coolant, or D_2O, leaking. The problem lay with why the heavy water was suddenly leaking, how much of it was leaking, and where it was leaking. There was no way to know. There was no manual back then, on how to deal with these types of problems. The control room fell into a panic. A veteran of nuclear power, manager Park Sang-ki, was also in a panicked state. At that fateful hour, one man saved the day. He was the director of the machinery division, Park Jae-jun.

"I will enter the hangar."

What a bolt out of the blue. To enter the hangar! He could die if something went wrong. If radiation were leaking, you would die in a few months, even with luck on your side. There was no way manager Park would let his subordinate enter. Moreover, he would have to answer to the safety committee, which had not approved this measure.

But the alarm unit kept on ringing, letting us know of a coolant leak (a leak of heavy water) at the power station, and several red lights flashed. The system of pressure tubes kept standing idle; if they didn't do something soon, then the tubes would soon break. Men stared at each other, at a loss for words. It was similar to a situation on a passenger plane; if the pilot had fainted, for example. There is only so much machinery can do to pinpoint a cause. A person must make the final discovery. The other Park, the director of the machinery division, again makes a request to enter the hangar. He gazes directly at the manager and the other co-manager.

"Isn't this the only way?" he asks.

His face showed dignified resolve, as if molded into stone. The other two lowered their heads. His bosses, Park and Kim, that is. Then after a long pause, the two nodded their heads. There are times when silence speaks louder than words.

The subordinate Park takes charge. He addresses the director of the Radiation Management Division.

"Please ring the alarm in five minute intervals. Once it rings four times, I will leave the hangar. Just in case I can't leave on my own, I am going to tie a rope around myself and enter," he said.

The maintenance personnel started bustling around busily. They gave him a hazmat suit to wear, along with a flashlight, a radiation detection instrument, and other tools. And so he entered. Was this Hell? Due to the hazy conditions within the hangar, he couldn't see very well. Alive or dead, what did this mean (in the greater scheme of things)? Life or death hangs in the balance, but it refers to others, and not his current predicament.

For himself there was no fear of death. Only one thing drove him forward. He had to find the cause. The steam coming from his surroundings turns his helmet foggy.

He couldn't see what lay in front of him. His hazmat suit is uncomfortable, and unwieldy. What use is the hazmat suit if he can't do his job properly? He rips it off and throws it to the side. Now he can see. The lower deck doesn't seem to have a problem. He starts climbing the stairs, counting as he goes. Finally, by the sixth floor, he finds something on the heavy water tank's exterior wall.

"Dear Lord!"

There is nothing wrong with the inner core.

"Let's get out of here!" He shouts to himself. He hurries. He's now frightened.

He clambers to the exit. He is soaked in heavy water. Like a ghost, he reappears in front of his fellow men. Other than the manager of the power plant, the others look at him with large, frightened eyes. Are they dreaming?

"I'm still alive and kicking!" He shouts. The others finally find their bearings.

His fellow men draw a long breath. Relief, sadness, joy, all these feelings intermingle. His boss, who has finally regained his senses, issues the order.

"There is no radiation leak. Go fix the wall of the heavy water tank."

"Qìzhǎnmǎsù"
(泣斬馬謖, Punishing the Favorite to Restore Order)

And so it went that we avoided, for the time being, at least, a major disaster. But the supposed accident could not be covered up like this. There was to be a complicated and arduous path towards restoring order. So what was the cause? Was it a natural disaster? Or was it a manmade disaster? Was the response appropriate? Were the proper safety regulations followed? What were the takeaway lessons from this? And so on and so forth. Of course, for the time being, once this became known, KEPCO was in an uproar, not to mention the South Korean government. Potential nuclear disasters are a scary thing, and rightfully so.

While the regional as well as national company headquarters were dealing with the fallout from this, officials from the Ministry of Energy and the Ministry of Science and Technology rushed to the scene. They are sure to try to assign the blame on someone, anyone. That much is clear. The site becomes chaotic. Instead of allotting the time to restoring the peace and dealing with fixing that damned heavy water tank wall, the workers are quick to protect me. If the government assigns blame, they are sure to blame the CEO. In other words, me. So they decided to keep it a secret from me. Stop chattering and listen, for a minute. They have to keep the peace.

The frightened head boss and his subordinates decided to hide the bravery of Park, who had entered the hangar at a great personal cost to himself. They decide to hide this from even me. Why? Because the proper safety protocols had not been followed. So they kept this secret for 30 years.

These men, what a chance they took on me.

During the 10 years that South Korea had been in the nuclear energy business, it was the first close call that we had. We had averted a literal meltdown of sorts, even though radiation had not been leaking. It was only natural that tensions were running high. From above, an order was issued to find the culprit and punish him. The majority of KEPCO was also on the offensive, and are all for punishing the parties involved. The damage done to the company was intangible, not just to its reputation but also to its credibility.

It also contradicted the mores behind my vision of an "Enertopia." Heavy water costs about $1,000 USD per kilo. It is more expensive than cognac. That is why leaking 30 tons of it caused a serious problem. We lost about 140 drums worth of heavy water. Not only this, but that was the least of our problems, because to make the plant operational again, it would take six months to a year. And how were we supposed to recoup the losses and find an alternative fuel source in the meantime?

The company headquarters wanted to clean up the mess at the Wolseong plant first. I flew to the site, accompanied by the senior vice president and the junior vice president. Thoughts raced through my mind during that plane ride. How could such an accident have happened? They (to my knowledge, then) were doing the best they could to undo the damage caused, but how could we punish the people involved at the plant? Not only this, but aside from the monetary costs, we would be sure to be met with censure over the safety of nuclear power, a loss of faith by the public in our company, and our trustworthiness as a whole. This was a debt that had to be paid. This was a horrendous event. I still cannot forgive them.

I arrived at the scene. The frightened men avoided eye contact, aside from the line up manager and the junior manager. Their shoulders were slumped, and it seemed as though the very breath of life had left their bodies. Why were they so silent and still?

I told everyone to assemble at the hall. About 300 workers at the site gathered, and everyone seemed to be hanging their heads. A heavy silence hung in the air. Armageddon. Was it here already?

As I contemplated this, another thought cropped up in my head. If the company morale fell to such straits, then we could surely not go on. But then again, I could not punish those involved. I can't forgive. I'm going to fire them. No. I will not be able to recoup the losses if I go down this route. I will lose people. I am shaken to my core. I am in a bind.

I was at a loss for words then looked at my workers again. The shoulders of my best and brightest, plant manager Park and his subordinate and popular boss Kim, are slumped. But are they not my company men?

This is when I remembered the tale of yesteryear, of "*eupcham masok*." How sad must the people of Zhuge Liang have been for Măsù, their favored one. But at the last, was he not slayed for the greater good and held accountable? I could not face myself if I didn't show more resolve. Wasn't this a true-life tale, handed down through generations of Koreans? I am flummoxed.

Do I fire these bosses? That would be punishment enough. But what good would this do? The company would suffer, lose people, lose its credibility, etc. I think the fate of Masok's untimely passing is not always the right answer. Fine. I will give them another chance.

"My beloved men, a person can fail, sometimes, and even make mistakes. The problem lies with 'how to fix that mistake.' Many of you have contributed to the company losing 50 billion KRW. You owe the company a debt. A great one. So pay it. I will give you a year. If you repay this debt, then I will not hold anyone accountable."

The hushed hall suddenly awoke with whispers. The men look at each other. They doubt their own ears.

"Just repay the debt?" They do not understand.

They had been expecting a scolding and salary reductions, because that was the correct order of things. But what was this? They were just told to "repay the debt." This left them flustered and confused. The executives stared at me as well, at a loss for words.

I say this now because I found out later that the subordinates of the manager of the power plant cried together that night like a real family.

"We will honor our promise." It appeared as though they had sworn an oath that night.

After that fateful night, the atmosphere of the power plant at Wolseong changed. The company men were always on the alert, always on the offensive, like soldiers always ready for battle. The razor-sharp tension in the air and their *jeongsung*, or deep earnestness swirled around the power plant for a whole year. They banded together around their leader and all 350 of them became as one.

A year passed. The British magazine, *Nuclear Engineering International*, rated the efficacy of the Wolseong Power Plant as first in the world. The Republic of Korea's Wolseong Power Plant Station 1 was the one where a big accident had taken place a year prior to this honor. At the time, there were 271 operational nuclear power plants in the world. Out of these, the Wolseong Power Plant marked a 98.4 percent efficacy rate, a truly remarkable record. This was ahead of even Canada, where they also used heavy water as a coolant and they had failed to surpass this record.

Here, to this day, stands a monument to mark this historic occasion.

There Are No Secrets

I cannot not talk more about this subject at hand. It is about section chief Park Jae-jun. That terrible day when we discovered the coolant leaking, Park displayed wisdom. But this secret was buried. Twenty-seven years passed.

It was in 2011 during the planning of the IAAF World Championships in Daegu. I was busy, as per usual. It was over 20 years since I had left KEPCO, but as I usually did, I invited some of the men from there to lunch. Some of the invitees included the head of the Daegu power plant, Cho Seong-hoon and Choi Mun-soo, the director of planning.

The topic that lay heavily on our minds that day was the disaster at the Fukushima Daiichi power plant that had happened some months before. I had read about the head of the power plant, Yoshida Masao, and his brave leadership, and he was the main topic of discussion. But at that moment, Choi said something that caught me off guard.

"President Park, during the Wolseong accident, there was another brave man who risked his life to enter the control room," he said.

"What?" I was so surprised.

A heavy silence followed.

"Repeat what you just said to me."

Silence again.

Oh no. This was supposed to be kept secret. That is what Choi realized with a start. What a mess. I am wearing a scary expression on my face.

"What do you mean, enter the reactor? I was the CEO back then. How can there be secrets that even the CEO doesn't know?"

"The truth is…"

There's no use crying over spilled milk. There's only one option left: to tell the truth.

He commences with his anecdote. His voice crawls to a whisper.

"At the time I was the director of the materials division and I was watching over Park the whole entire time. When the accident happened, everyone was at a loss over what to do. Park entered the hangar willingly and wrapped a rope around his body and made the discovery [that the coolant was leaking]."

"What?"

My mouth drops open.

How can such a secret have been kept in broad daylight? And his righteous act kept from me for about 30 years?

That such an event had occurred under my tenure as CEO at KEPCO. I couldn't contain my temper.

"Arrange a meeting with Park immediately." I was very angry.

"Yes, sir."

Choi responded in a small voice.

About a week later, I was finally able to meet Park.

“So you are the one!” I am too shaken to speak.

My head grew hot. He had made the trip from the port city of Ulsan, down south. We look at each other and start laughing. A million emotions, as the saying goes in Korea, cross my mind. He must have felt the same. Words weren’t necessary.

After meeting him, I couldn’t sit still. I wanted to repay him somehow. I wanted to elevate his status. But this, alas, was out of my reach as I had already left the company. I was sorry.

A few days later, I met the then-CEO Kim Ssang-soo. I explained what had happened at Wolseong years ago.

He was so alarmed by this news that his mouth gaped open as well.

“I understand,” he said.

His response was brief and to the point. I say this again, but a really effective CEO stands apart from the pack. He had made his career at one of the biggest Korean conglomerates, LG. He was the first CEO at KEPCO who had been selected from a private enterprise. The reason why a new wave of change had occurred at KEPCO was thanks to him. He modernized the place. Kim also played an instrumental role in securing contracts in the UAE during his tenure.

July 1, 2011. It was the 50th anniversary of the Korea Electric Power Corporation’s founding. Park was awarded, along with nine other employees who had made a huge contribution to the development of the company. Among the recipients were Lim Han-que and Chung Geon, the chiefs of the department for nuclear engineering independence and new business ventures.

We tend to value a society that delivers justice, but sometimes, this golden rule doesn’t apply. A society that recognizes and rewards hard work is a good one too. Park should have been honored right away, but his bravery was only recognized about 30 years later. I am deeply moved and saddened at the same time. What a shame.

So it goes that one man's brave deed only came to light exactly 27 years later. Dare I say, I am also relieved that Lim Han-que and Chung Geon's achievements toward the development of future nuclear power businesses were recognized at the same ceremony.

CHAPTER 10

The 10th Asian Games

The CEO Must Run

In September 1986, South Korea came to host the 10th Asian Games. Until this point, it had been the home to many international competitions, but all of them had been for a single sport or event. An international competition spanning multiple events and sports had never been pulled off on the Korean peninsula. In 1970, we had tried to host the 6th Asian Games but had to pull out, making this new achievement no small feat.

The government made a survey of the actual conditions of sports organizations before the Games. Unfortunately for us, they were in various states of disrepair. The federal government immediately made amends by assigning each sporting event to a large corporation. POSCO was assigned gymnastics, Hyundai, swimming, Samsung, wrestling, etc. KEPCO became responsible for track and field events. This was back in January 1985.

Along with this assignment, as the head of the Korea Electric Power Corporation, I decided to do my own personal survey of track and field events. Alas, the problems we faced were many. One of the biggest problems was the lack of ability in many of our athletes. Track and field is the fairest of all events, in my opinion. It is all about setting records. New ones. It is different from those mediated by referees. Every new record is mandated, exactly to the millisecond, by the clock.

Track and field athletes cannot outpace their abilities in a short period of time. There was only one year before the Games. There were 45 events, and many medals that were for the winning. KEPCO felt its responsibility deeply.

With the commencement of our newly found role, we pulled in many track and field experts and coaches, and made plans. To increase endurance and ability, there is no better way than to train and train hard. Before the Games, we decided to use the time to the best of our abilities, and train very, very, hard, that had never been seen before in our nation's history.

About six months into training, we started tracking records. Maybe I was too hasty, but the records of our athletes fell short of my expectations. I raised the bar even higher for them. The hastier you are, turn back (and start at the beginning) as the saying goes, but if you get it wrong, you'll just give lazy people an excuse. You have to make the right judgment call in these types of situations.

When it comes to training, "military style" is best. It is like preparing for battle. How efficient would this be? The reason why we fail is because we fail to "properly" do something.

I only oversaw whether things were running "properly." At this, there were sometimes uproar and roars of dissent. You cannot let these things go. I pushed them even harder. If they complained, I kicked them out. Sweat and hard work pays off in the end, in an increase of ability.

You have to experience hardships in order to unite. This also increases the morale. The commonplace "ok, ok," is sometimes thought to raise the morale, but this is a mistaken belief. In order to pick yourself up after falling and win over hardship, you have to push yourself. Only organizations that push themselves, almost to the breaking point, are the ones who succeed in the end.

Sometimes it seems as though they are doing it "properly," but the results aren't worth mentioning. I was very concerned. I thought they were doing things correctly, but why wasn't their strategy working? If "properly" doesn't work, then wasn't there no other methods worth pursuing? My concerns grew.

A year passed, very quickly at that. There were really no real records that were set. The second-rate athletes' abilities were growing, but the first-rate athletes were at a standstill, or so it seemed. We could only win medals if the first-rate athletes did well—but as they were experiencing a slump, it really made me uneasy.

In track and field events, the projected win was in only one event—the men's 200 m. South Korean sprinter Jang Jae-geun. An Asian champion. A record of 20.41 seconds. Back then he was the fastest in his group in Asia.

During the past year, I believed that if the athletes trained "properly" or "correctly," they would succeed, but they fell short of my expectations. I did not forecast a gold medal in any event other than the 200 meters. But the South Korean government imposed a new goal of at least two gold medals in each event. I immediately objected. Our current abilities would only win us one gold; I asked them to lower these expectations. I even reported the past year's results. If I had more time, we may have had more hope, but I said expecting more than one exceeded even my boldest dreams.

The athletic department was adamant. "There are 45 events. What do you mean, only one gold medal? There must be at least two."

I couldn't help but object again.

"Who wants just one gold medal? The past year, we have trained harder and harder, but our abilities only amount to this, so isn't this the only way?"

The Ministry of Culture and Sports was adamant.

"No excuses. Two golds or else." The nail on the coffin. My objections grew louder.

"KEPCO was tasked with an impossible job. Only one gold medal is possible at this point. Other associations, they were not assigned a goal that is twice that of what is possible! What are you to say after the Games are held?"

The Ministry was immovable.

In truth, there were 45 gold medals for the winning in the track and field events, and asking us for two gold medals was a blow to my pride. But what was I to do? If "properly" didn't work? My insides churned.

About 100 days before the Asian Games, the Ministry of Culture and Sports decided to hold a briefing about the upcoming Games. At the time, Lee Young-ho (a close personal friend of mine) was the minister of this particular ministry. I was close to tears as I imagined the public humiliation of it. But what to do? It was out of my hands.

On the day of the briefing, the South Korean President, along with the heads of many ministries and the leaders of the opposition party, Kim Young-sam and Kim Dae-jung, were both invited. Other people of repute were also to be in attendance. Wouldn't the public be so upset that a big corporation such as KEPCO was only capable of winning two golds? My thoughts grew weary.

At last, the meeting started. Swimming, boxing, gymnastics, wrestling, etc. were all called in order, and the number of projected golds presented. Finally, the track and field association was called.

"Two golds!" Said the director of planning with confidence.

I rose unexpectedly and raised my hand.

"Our track and field association, due to mitigating circumstances, can only win one gold in the upcoming Asian Games."

I felt like I was talking to all those assembled, and clarifying my and consequently, KEPCO's, stance. All eyes turned towards me. The auditorium started to stir. The planning director turned a ghastly shade of white. Minister Lee turned to me with his eyes narrowed. The auditorium turned quiet and still. It seemed as though time had stopped. It seemed as though a person could not rise and speak. Only a few minutes passed.

But after what seemed like forever, President Chun Doo-hwan said, "Then you, CEO Park, must run!"

Wow—the auditorium filled with laughter. The awkward moment passed. It was a well-intentioned order. But it was a frightening order, nonetheless.

The auditorium became quiet again, and the meeting commenced.

But I was in dire straits. South Korean President Chun had only been half-joking. KEPCO's goals then really cemented into earning two gold medals, and the problem was that I might really have to run.

I was just protesting. Then look at what ended up happening; I was filled with trepidation at my new order. Others had laughed, but I was serious. Two golds were impossible. I had seen this throughout the last year. And they had trained "properly." I was filled with a sense of dread. There were no days hence when I didn't worry, and days passed without a clear solution.

"Properly" had not worked, and I was filled with disappointment. You cannot achieve things easily in this life, is what I realized. I became lost in thought.

Why Worry When You Can Pray?

I passed some days in anguish. The Games would open soon, and the athletes under my care were not setting new records, and I might even have to run (literally). I was physically and mentally exhausted.

In addition, because "properly" had not worked, I was disappointed in myself. Why wasn't this working? The coaches and the athletes had done their best to train properly. I fell deep into thought. What was the problem? Where was the weak point? I was waiting for a solution.

Then my disarrayed thoughts stopped. Of course. I had rushed it. I should have given them more time. Because I was so rushed, I had pushed them too hard. Not only this, but there were other variables that came into play. I realized that I had been torturing both the coaches and the athletes. But what was this? Everything in life takes time to reach fruition. In terms of endurance, it shows up after the passage of time. And this meant that I would have to go back and use wisdom.

I needed to give them time, suppress my harried state, and wait for them to improve with a less burdened heart. I hadn't worked "properly."

This was because I had been pushing them too hard. But what to do. The 10th Asian Games was looming close.

One day, I was on my way to Gwacheon, when I passed by a nearby church. Near it, near the bell steeple, was inscribed in big letters, "Why worry when you can pray?" I suddenly felt like I'd been struck by a bolt of lightning.

"Prayers," I muttered to myself. But of course! Why worry? My heart beat a little bit faster. Of course. There's always prayer.

The next day, near sunrise, I called my driver to arrange a trip to the nearby sports auditorium. As it is still dark, the security guard blocks us from entering. This is because ahead of the Games, the South Korean government had installed a police presence. This is because from the beginning, as soon as we announced we were opening the Games, North Korea had been troublesome.

I asked the security guard for a reprieve and went inside. I ran one lap around the track. Then I went around the high pole vault, and the long jump area, to the stadium's stands. I gazed far away, at the sky. It seemed as though the sunrise was far away. I bowed my head, and prayed. I prayed with all my heart and all my soul. I prayed for the athletes, that they would fight well, and I also prayed for my company's honor.

The next day found me at the same place, repeating the same routine. And the next, and the next. About a fortnight passed. I was met by someone I didn't know. He greeted me warmly. He was a government official. "He must have gotten the word from my subordinates," I thought. I returned his greeting.

We sat together at the stands. Enveloped in the dark, we gazed far ahead of us, towards the horizon. The sun was not yet up. Dimly, I could see Namhansanseong Fortress ahead of us.

The Deputy Commissioner General (the head of the Korean National Police Agency) was a man of a few words. Sitting together in the bleachers like that, an understanding passed between us.

At first, he must have taken the junior police officer's report and must have allowed the exception. However, if I came so early to the stadium, even as the KEPCO chief, he must have thought it was strange. As if I didn't have enough to do.

"Who is it? What does he do?" He must have asked pointed questions. He must have conducted a background check. Then he would have felt the severity of the situation that I was facing.

He must have endured many trials until he reached his current position, I thought. A few days prior, there had been an explosion at Gimpo International Airport. A spy had thrown a bomb into a trashcan. Many people had died.

In about a fortnight, the stadium would be filled with more than 80,000 athletes from all over Asia. There is no way of knowing what unexpected accidents lay in store. As such, if another terrorist attack occurred, then it would be a big mess. I thought to myself that his worries must be greater than mine.

In the dark, we sat there, with responsibility weighing heavily on both our shoulders. A heavy silence lay between us. The vista grew hazy. I was gazing at the nearby fortress, somewhat off in the distance. Was the sun about to rise?

"The sky's fair today."

I broke the silence. I meant it in a spirit of solidarity, but the phrase came out awkwardly.

“Thank you,” he replied.

Another awkward and strange response. But you, dear reader, know this: our hearts had spoken. I was not the only one who felt overburdened. We call this “*dongbyung sangryun*,” in Korean, or that there is shared sympathy for those in similar straits. We took comfort in each other. We two sat together for a long while, without speaking. I felt comforted.

Up until the opening of the Games, I visited the stadium every single day. Time waits for no man. For people who are in a rush, time passes even faster. The Games loomed ominously in the not-so-distant future. My worries, despite my prayers, grew tenfold.

About a fortnight before the opening ceremony, a teacher from Sungbo Girls’ High School, Kim Beon-il, came to visit me. He turned out to be a Godsend. He mentioned that he had a female student, Lim Chun (Lim Chun-ae). She was only in her second year at the high school, but her time at the 800-meter dash was improving rapidly. Her speed wasn’t yet up to par with the fastest female Asian athletes such as China’s Yang Liuxia; however, about a month earlier, she had been playing catch-up at a frightening speed. We call this “*sangseung gokseon*,” or a rising curve, in Korean. Her coach and mentor told me that it might be worthwhile to have her compete in the upcoming Asian Games. Lim was one of the rising star athlete-scholars that KEPCO had been sponsoring in their “Dream Tree” philanthropic endeavors. She was one of 50 students across the nation that was receiving 300,000 KRW every month.

And so it goes that Lim would eventually clinch the other gold medal along with Jang Jae-geun (him in the 200-meter dash). I did not know this at the time. But I was so relieved! I wouldn’t literally have to run in an event myself. The power of prayer is a wonderful thing. And that it would have such quick results! I was much moved.

"Teacher Kim, Chun-ae should not be placed with the other athletes at the athlete village. She's our [golden goose]. I don't want anyone to know about her [before the start of the Games]," I said.

I made my plea thusly. We needed to hide our dark horse. Until the day of the event, we decided to house her at the Korean National Training Center instead. If we placed her with the others, it would be difficult to hide her talents from everyone else.

Lim's time in the sun finally came. On my way to the event, one of my private secretaries, Kim Mun-kyung, glanced into the rear view mirror and said to me, "President Park, I see a gold medal for [South Korea] today."

"What?" Kim did not know about Lim, did he? I was caught off-guard.

"Where did you hear such news?"

"I am sorry, but there's someone that I've been seeing."

"Who?"

"Oh, I am sorry to say I have to keep it a secret." My interest was piqued.

"Who is this person?"

After some time, he said, "He is a monk."

"What? A monk?" My head started to steam.

"Turn around. I need to get to the office instead."

As soon as I arrived at the office, I called Kim to my office again.

"Tell me everything! From beginning to end!"

He began to explain. There was a monk that he was fond of, and he had the gift of sight, or clairvoyance. A few days ago, he had visited him, and he had said to him, "Your boss has another gold medal in the works." I was so surprised. I was so, so, very very happy. I guessed we really would show them quite a time. My temper subsided.

"Where can I find this monk? For later?" I asked.

This was such a relief to me. I was excited too. But of course. I had done the right thing. I had done things "properly," after all. But I am getting ahead of myself. Let us race ahead to the day of the event again.

A new record is about to be set. In the women's 800-meter dash, there are eight finalists. One of them will win the race. Of course, Lim has to win. My heart feels like it's being squeezed. I can't breathe.

Far off in the distance, I can see the slender Lim. She is from a financially disadvantaged family, and I have heard that she was raised on ramen. But this was a story fabricated by the media. She had beef, and she also had snake soup. I can see her crowned as the next Yang Liuxia.

"Chun-ae, please beat Yang. There's no need to pay attention to the others. Run. Run and run and run," I whispered in my head.

With the sound of a gunshot, they're off and running. The final eight rush off like pistols. During the first 400 meters, they are like a pack. It's hard to distinguish between them. They have to run two laps around the stadium. With one lap left, Liuxia is leading all of them. Where is Chun-ae? She's right behind her.

"You're doing well," I say to myself.

When she passes the 500-meter mark, the eight are now separated, with two leading the rest. Well, to be honest, four of them are in the lead, and four are trailing. And then out of the last four, the last two start lagging behind. And out of the fastest four, they also start separating. They pass the 600-meter mark. They start increasing their speed. The 700-meter mark. Only three are in the lead now. They start running even faster. They are running like the wind. Liuxia, Lim, then India's Shiny Kurisingal

Abraham. Only a step or two divides them. They are only 20 meters from the finish line. 15 meters, 10 meters, and the top three's ranking doesn't change.

My heart feels like it's about to explode. Only 5 meters left. I cannot believe what is happening. Lim passes Liuxia. I stand up. Lim is first. She's in first place! I feel like I can't see any more.

"Wow. Wow!" The stadium erupts in cheers. I feel like the stadium is about to explode. I'm about to explode. They are pumping their fists in the air. Some are clambering and pushing those right ahead of them down, to see better. Where am I? Who are you? Why are we screaming? There is no me, there is no you. There is only Lim, who just won. 5 meters, 3 meters, 2 meters. Damn it!

India's in the lead. India wins! First place, India! Second place, Chun-ae! Third place, Liuxia!

I closed my eyes. Then I breathed deeply, in and out. I sigh in consternation. No, this is not the end. It's not the end all and be all. I feel like the sky is falling in pieces all around me. And I feel helpless. I stand up again, without a word. As others hurriedly greet me goodbye, I want to escape even faster. I hurry. I wanted to leave this place as soon as possible.

Some of the bleachers are void of people. The most important race, perhaps, for them, was now over. There is no place on Earth where the air was crackling moments before, with electricity. I move to a corner, and sit. I feel gravity pushing me down. I am at a loss for words. Everyone who knows me avoids me like the plague. My eyes are closed. How empty do I feel? That we were robbed of our medal!

How much time has passed? The track and field's Lee Kyu-seop, the assistant director-general, comes for me.

"President Park." At first, I can't hear him. "President Park!" I open my eyes.

"Um…that is…" He hesitates.

"What!" I respond curtly.

"That is…"

"Tell me quickly!" Lee was trapped.

"I just told you, tell me at once!"

"The Indian athlete, she was disqualified!"

"What? Disqualified?" I was jolted wide-awake.

"If [the Indian athlete] was disqualified, then do you mean Chun-ae is in first place?"

"I just said so!"

"Then you should have told me immediately, instead of hesitating."

This was an unnecessary remark. I was over the moon. It was the principle of the thing. I felt like I was flying.

"There, there, now tell me the whole story." My attitude had changed.

According to the assistant director general, "The Indian athlete had already entered another athlete's lane before the running breakthrough, thereby…[becoming] disqualified.•"

"Then there must be some evidence."

"I have prepared the taped race for your perusal."

"Then turn it on. Before the rest of the people in the bleachers leave."

The tape was played in the stadium. The commentator's voice boomed

• In the 800-meter race, an athlete must run the full 400-meters (the first of two laps) before entering another person's lane. The Indian athlete entered Lane 1 (before her lap was done), thereby becoming disqualified.

over the loudspeakers. The Indian athlete had been disqualified, and her mistake was shown on the large TV screens.

"Waaah." The audience roared.

After clinching the gold, Lim went on to win two other golds, sweeping the 1,500 meter as well as the 3,000 meter races. What a marvelous achievement! This became the first triple-crown event in the history of modern Asian athletics. This was not all. Our track and field events won us South Koreans four more medals, contributing to the total number of golds: seven. For South Korea, it was a proud moment in our long-storied history.

This was not all. In the 1992 Barcelona Olympics, Hwang Young-cho won the gold in the men's marathon. In the 1996 Atlanta Olympics, Lee Bong-ju won the silver in the same event. In 2011, Daegu, South Korea came to host one of the big three athletics events in the world; the IAAF World Championships. After the designation of Stuttgart, Germany as the first of the world athletics cities, Daegu came to claim the same title. Thirty years into the making, and the IAAF knew without a doubt that Daegu put on quite a show. This was quite an undertaking that even London, Berlin, and Moscow failed to do.

Such is the power of prayer.

CHAPTER 11

An Exciting Place to Work, A Life Worth Living for: KEPCO

Corporate Philosophy

A corporation is called a corporate body for a reason. The heart may not beat but it has the same personality and the same philosophy throughout the various divisions. It also must have class. National dignity and a sense of personal human dignity are also other examples of what I am about to address.

A corporation must have a reason behind its various workings. The values and goals of a company must have noble aims. This is why management principles and management philosophies emerge, and the employees' codes of conduct should comply with these principles and philosophies to create the "company culture."

In the early 1980s, there were no terms to describe "corporate culture," or "corporate philosophy." "Management philosophies," and "management principles," were widely discussed instead. Large conglomerates were surviving by overstretching themselves, and to survive, they were only following the money; in other words, seeking profits. "People-centric," "Respecting the dignity of the human during business dealings," are terms that became popular after the early 1980's. This was a time when businesses were not focusing on the corporate body.

But KEPCO, I believe, had to be different. The pursuit of profits are important goals to focus on at first. But the company's societal role must also be taken into account.

As I grew to know KEPCO better, I realized that the corporation's business dealings could not be treated the same way. I believed that KEPCO's ability to provide a high-quality supply of electricity to a larger number of households and businesses in a safer, more affordable, and more effective way, would become the cornerstone of a more affluent society. I also believed that KEPCO's vision of an "Enertopia" would save South Korea from an energy-depleted state. KEPCO's mission and importance for the country of South Korea, as a state-owned and state-operated company, is the reason why it still exists today.

All throughout the Republic of Korea, every citizen used to be our customer and user. There was no one else to rely on but KEPCO. In 1983, for example, KEPCO's yearly operating budget amounted to almost half the national budget of 10.4 trillion won, and approached 10 percent of the GDP. How meaningful is a company like this?

Electricity is the simplest and the most affordable type of energy. And it is also cleaner. The problem lies in its cost; it's a little bit more expensive to produce. Electricity drives our modern day lives. We can live without cars, but without electricity, our refrigerators, as well as the elevators, halt to a stop. The TV and telephones stop working. A comfortable living, and an affluent society, cannot be imagined without modern-day electricity. Electricity's function and role contributes to the betterment of human society.

So it follows that I instituted the "development of a nuclear energy culture." KEPCO's brilliant ace, Lee Bong-rae, was responsible for making sure this culture came to fruition. While the ideal of an "enertopia" is a noble one, it is an ideology and cannot be put into practice in our current society. Thus, we must take one step at a time towards this goal. It may seem within our grasp at times, but oh, how elusive!

History is the product of solidarity.• You may even simplify it further by calling it fate. The relationship between God and man, the interplay between man and nature, and relationships between man and fellow man, create episodes that all contribute to the annals of history. Can religion exist without the relationship between man and God? Man has no "relationship," per se, with nature; however, nature and the universe continue to spin on. A mountain is still a mountain without humans, like a field or a plain, and stars continue to wander across the night sky. A man without relationships is solitary, without societal and cultural contributions to make.

The development of culture comes about as interplay between the ideal and reality. The nascent "nuclear energy culture" comes from the interplay between the company, KEPCO, and its users. As the interplay between reality and the ideal starts, it is important to maintain the solidarity between KEPCO and its compatriots. So how to begin this relationship? It is through trust and love. Trust and love comes through service. The service is endless, and must continue to the very end. Through a mental, mutually beneficial relationship, trust and love prevail. This relationship between

• *"Yeondaeron,"* is a newly coined term that I have invented in a previous book, titled, *Plain Stories by a Grandpa on Civilization*.

KEPCO and its users should not end after paying the electric bill at the end of every month. Rather, its users should feel "trust and love for KEPCO."

Should only KEPCO wear the crown when it comes to being beloved? No. Samsung should be loved, and LG should be loved and trusted as well. As there are people and as there are corporations, these aforementioned conglomerates of South Korea have relationships with the consumers of their products. Can you imagine a corporation without any consumers?

The complex interplay between consumers and a corporation, should it fail, will bring about problems such as environmental concerns, a rapidly aging population, and other societal ills. There will be no end in sight. Every corporation must build a relationship with their consumers, with love and trust as their backbone.

What is the ultimate goal of a corporation? To make the world a better place.

KEPCO's sponsorship of youth football players is an excellent way to communicate our corporation's enduring legacy for the years to come. It is the "*yeondae*" between company and consumers. "The electric energy grand prize" awarded to KEPCO by the mass media is another such example. Love and trust through youth football, and communication and encouragement through the mass media, will contribute to the development of culture. Unfortunately, one of my successors has done away with the football sponsorships recently. And one media outlet reneged on its social promise and trashed a system it was supposed to nurture.

Of course, the merging of businesses is important. But it's also of vital importance that our countrymen get excited (about something). This ensures that the state's honor also rises with the rest. If you are at KEPCO's level, at the very least, you should gaze at the sun, hiding above the clouds. The

Korea Electric Power Corporation is forever entwined with history. Upon hearing this, let us remember ourselves, past and present. Now let us turn our gaze to the new world, dawning near the horizon.

What Is the Problem?

As a state-owned, state-operated corporation, KEPCO stands firmly on strong foundations, ensuring its status amongst electric power companies. It is a giant amongst giants. However, if it faces no competitors and does not have external stimuli, a company will lose its vitality. KEPCO, I'm afraid, has turned into an obsolete dinosaur.

What was our main problem? We have sinned with our too-proud thoughts. This is how the world views us. So what do we need? Something called "*euisik gaehyuk*" in Korean, or reforming the consciousness. We must breathe life into Consciousness of History, and realize KEPCO's partnership with History, and race towards the ideal of an "Enertopia."

So it follows that in 1983, when I was first appointed as the chief executive officer of KEPCO, I made the company slogan, "Vibrant KEPCO." In 1984, I changed the slogan to "Trust and Love, KEPCO," and played an important role in instilling the company as a state-owned corporation with an interest in benefiting the public. In 1985, it was "An Exciting Place To Work, A Life Worth Living For: KEPCO." Finally, in 1986, I changed the unofficial slogan to "Shaping the Future, Classy KEPCO." The slogans were just that, slogans, or another synonym for the company at large. That is why "move to action, find a path," became another hidden company mantra.

In 1985, we upgraded the company's external image via a CIP, or Capital Improvement Plan, and sponsored a rugby team to instill in KEPCO a spirit of sacrifice and "fighting." This was all towards the development of a "pioneering spirit" amongst our beloved employees.

We started a campaign dubbed "MV," meaning Management Vitality, since 1986. This MV campaign was designed to speed up management achievements, and it was modeled after a principle of what can be translated into a "micro group management," which began in the late 1970s in Germany. Under this project, the whole workforce of the corporation was organized into small groups with no more than 10 members each, and therefore there were a total 1500-plus small groups. Then we had each group discuss urgent issues in its own territory. What was discussed varied from management policies of the leader to other urgent projects.

The MV movement's biggest asset is communication. "Learn together, share ideas together, and work together." This is the backbone of Management Vitality. If you sit at the desk of the CEO and just issue orders, then it may come as a surprise to you that it becomes like neighborhood gossip; it may become catastrophic. We should hold brainstorming sessions and examine even the CEO's ideas. Then they will be able to understand the mindset of a leader of the corporation. "Aha, that's what he meant," they would say.

Through the brainstorming session, the employees of the company should get their messages from the executives of the company, including the CEO himself. The subordinates then can also be able to convey their ideas and thoughts to the executives, giving them real time updates about the types of situations and problems that they were facing. A company that is based on mutual trust, and compassion between each employee, regardless of rank, and where the executives engage freely with the other employees, lends itself to a successful, energetic enterprise.

An Exciting Workplace

Whether you succeed or fail in life is determined at your workplace. You realize your dreams and goals, and you make your contribution to the society through your job. It is estimated that a person spends about a third of the day at his place of employment. This place is also where human bonds are made. Sometimes, this is the place where battles are fought, a place where your dreams come to fruition, a place where you feel deeply moved, and also a place where you cry at times. Where will you find the "fun" in life unless you find it in your workplace? A happy family home, a bright society, and a strong nation must have employees that are happy at work, where they feel a zest for life. So it follows that we should make these workplaces a happy place to work.

This goes far beyond business ideology. A healthy body and a healthy mind contribute to a healthy organization and this noble spirit becomes imbued in everyone to really create a "fun" company culture. Without ideologies, there are other things that command our attention from time to time, but these come from working hard at work. These perks include a nice home and a salary. The workplace is also a place where friendships are formed, and promotions are found. A CEO to admire is also present here.

When I was appointed CEO at KEPCO, my inauguration was held at a subsidiary auditorium. I was not particularly ashamed. I did not have any regrets. But I had one thing in mind. One thing that I was determined to fix, while I was touring around the country. It was the rundown status of the corporation's building. They say that "Fine feathers make fine birds." Your neighbors judge you by what you wear. This is a saying from the West.

In 1983, during my first round of visits at the regional subsidiaries of KEPCO, I visited Gyeongju, the storied city filled with ancient history. There is a spirit of warmth in this city that I have never encountered anywhere else. Beautiful Korean-style houses, or *hanok*, *bibimbap* with bean sprouts, and a general calmness pervaded through the city and pulled my heart towards it. But when we finally reached the company building of our destination, I was appalled. It was so old. It felt like I was viewing the failing grades of a child. How awful. When I was inaugurated as the CEO of KEPCO, I had shouted, "KEPCO, the lively company!" Didn't I start off by saying "walk energetically?" I told these kind people to lead with their chests, but the company had not done enough for them.

Upon return to my office, I immediately called the executive who was in charge to make a report on the circumstances of the corporation building in general. Our "feathers" were just too tattered. Yes, I know, clothes are not the be all and end all of a person, and a company's public visage, literally, is not all. However, imagine a child holding his father's hand, and walking past this dilapidated building. How is the father supposed to point at the building, and say, "Son, this is where I work." I couldn't bear to see this possible occurrence happen over and over again. I could imagine the shame of the father, and of his wife. When a wife feels excitement and the son becomes proud of the breadwinner of the family (back then it was really customary for men to shoulder the burden of putting food on the table), is when the husband becomes really happy. KEPCO's in the black, so why did they not renovate the place? Even the unofficial slogan that I had been implementing across all the locations of KEPCO, which loosely translates to "The Energetic KEPCO Movement," was not being put to use. I immediately thought this could not do.

I was determined to live up to the upcoming slogans like "An exciting place to work, the beloved KEPCO" and "Frontrunner KEPCO." And this meant that we also need to polish the looks. We needed to start working on the renovations of the offices around the country.

The Jeonju regional office building began construction in 1983, and was finished by 1985, when the employees were finally able to move in. During the planning phases, at the new office building, we decided to get rid of the fences. A tall wall would be detrimental to the consumers and how could we communicate with them otherwise? This was the first time that a state-owned company did not have walls barricading them from the public. The employees must have been proud of this moment. Actions, not theories, move people.

The Gwangju office, which sits in the magnificent city of the Honam area, was built in an ultramodern style, just like the speed of the progress that the city was making. It was designed by Professor Kim Jin-gyun, who was also an architect of the Gangneung office.

There is another building I would like to mention. It is the KEPCO regional headquarters in Gyeongju. In 1985, the city of Gyeongju underwent gentrification and redevelopment, the likes of which had never been seen before. We had to obtain special permission from the city government to obtain new land for our regional office; in 1985, because of a redevelopment plan of the Gyeongju city government, the region's KEPCO office had to be relocated. We asked the city government to take extra care in giving us a new venue, and we were given the spot right next to the Wolseong county office as the new office land. I was lightly disappointed to see the county office building. Gyeongju is a city that was designated as a World Heritage Site, by the UNESCO. Then buildings for public offices should be designed up to par to that status of such a city. But the county office was built not with such a care. Of course there must have been a budget issue. But you cannot say that enough budget directly leads to a nice building. Even with a tight budget, you can build dignity. Only if you care. Attention is what it takes.

"KEPCO will show them," I thought. I returned to Seoul and called the head of the management-planning department and told him to design the new Gyeongju office in a traditional Korean hanok style. I told him to style it in the manner of a traditional Korean house, or *hanok*. KEPCO undertook this project in 1986, and it took three years for it to be built. It stands, to this day, as one of the finest examples of architecture, fit for the long-storied, legendary city of Gyeongju.

Not long ago, I heard a sad tale. The Samseong-dong office was going to be sold, and by November, moved to Naju. Samseong-dong's office was designated as the "best office building in [South] Korea" in 1987, by the Seoul metropolitan government a year after it was built and the employees moved in. Architecture is art. It marries functionality and beauty. If the functionality fails, then employees will be upset, and if it is ugly, then it will affect the beauty of the city. Don't people from all over the world visit Paris, France?

A building's age is over 100 years old (there). The people who live there, as well as the visitors, take delight in its beauty. If it is renovated badly or torn down, then it harms even the descendants. This is something that building owners should take into account.

A company's headquarters may be limited by what it looks like on the outside, but within it, the exterior landscaping and arrangement of artworks must also be pleasing. This, however, was out of my bounds. I went to the CEO of *Seoul Shinmun*, Mun Tae-gap, who was a man of great insight and highly intelligent. He assembled for me a team of artists. The art world's Oh Seung-woo, who was noted for his paintings. Another great figure in Western-style painting, Oh Ji-ho, was his father. The younger Oh hated being called someone's son, but that's how I always called him.

When you enter "Hanbit Hall," you can see the painting on the wall, titled, *Paradise*. At first, his painting was deemed too radical and avant-garde, so it underwent three revisions. I wonder if this may have interfered with the original piece. Some people still say the painting is too creepy.

For sculptures, we had Kim Young-joong, a professor from Hongik University. In the lobby, we have Kim's wall relief. The *Love for Mankind* sculpture in the garden is the product of professor Choi Ki-won, also from Hongik University.

Another sculpture, titled *Dynamic* was originally a 10-meter-high steel chimney, which was an exhaust pipe of the building. It was not pretty at all, and everyone frowned at it. I had it fixed, and it was reborn as an artwork. Professor Kim Young-joong and Professor Kwon Soon-hyung joined hands to create this artwork.

The most beautiful part of the headquarters, in my view, is the pine tree garden. It was, to my knowledge, one of the few times where a 3,000 *pyeong*, large pine tree garden was planted in Seoul.

We brought 12 of these trees, each over 200 years old, and mixed them with about 250 medium to smaller-sized trees. We got rid of the fence, and we mixed them with one of the main roads at Samseong-dong. It became a garden not just for KEPCO, but for the people as well.

For the landscaping, we took into account all four seasons and paid close attention to bringing delight to everyone during spring, summer, fall, and winter. We carefully considered the types of trees and flowers that were planted at the site. Upon the company headquarters moving to Naju, I will always miss the bright reddish pink blossoms of the azaleas located here.

Towards the southern gate, there are ten juniper trees that have lived for over 100 years. These trees had been procured with difficulty, and it had taken Shin Seon-gyun, the head of HR, over a year to find all of them. It is not easy to find ten juniper trees around the same age to plant together as a grove. As such, everyone had contributed in some way to create this beauty, these company headquarters we had here.

All things came to fruition, one by one, to create a whole. Each project may have been completed separately, but as a whole, they came together harmoniously. This is why our company headquarters became a step above the rest.

Within the Seoul metropolitan area, there are many fine buildings, but they do not create a harmonious whole. Of course, this is not the fault of the buildings' owners. It is due to the failures of the city's planning committee, and the failure of the South Korean government.

Well, I do have to admit that there are some others with bad taste. This example is from over 30 years ago, but I have seen a dead tree in front of some conglomerate's building. This juniper tree that I mention was located near Seosomun-dong, and they left it to die for months. A building is not just for ownership's sake. A city should be beautiful, and this sense of responsibility and type of thinking will place Seoul a notch above the rest. This is the responsibility of the noblesse oblige.

There is another concern that worries me. It is to do with the buildings' owners. They are solely concerned with how high their buildings will be. In the West, they are always concerned, even when a shopping mall is about to be built in the suburbs. But we Seoulites seem not to care if we drag a large-scale shopping mall into the city. This is not just an eyesore but also a headache inducing. It paralyzes the transportation and causes traffic, and the energy needed to keep this mall going is an intangible type of loss called, "*yuhyung muhyung*," in Korean. This is a waste of national power, in my opinion.

I took the responsibility for picking the venue for the *Statue of the KEPCO Employee*, which is a symbol of Enertopia. I followed a professor of Seoul National University who knew well about feng shui. This place was where my ideal of an "Enertopia" would be realized and come to fruition. Feng shui is art distilled into a science, and has roots in Asia. The professor stuck a rod into the garden's soil, and walked ten steps from the rod and said to me, the commemorative statue can be placed anywhere near this circumference. Using this rule would ensure an auspicious location, he said.

We placed a rod where the monument would be placed and we moved it about, trying to see from where it would look best. We viewed it from the CEO's office, and from the ground floor, and from the top of the building.

We also looked at it from where the rod was placed, where it gazed at the main building. We needed to figure out where sculpture should be placed. It took us a month. It took us this long as we moved the stake about. After placing it in what we thought was its final resting place, we sought the advice of the company's executives. But what was this! The auditor, Park Chun-geo, said to me, place it five steps away from the current location.

"I've thought about this for a month," I said.

"It could have taken you 10 months instead of a month, and still, something that is invisible will still remain invisible," he said.

"What do you mean?" I asked. I implied that he was being rude.

"It may sound rude to you, and discourteous, but I mean to say it anyway," he said.

"You sound sure of yourself."

"We can even place a bet on it."

"Look at this fellow. What is he guessing at?" I wondered. But I couldn't give in to him.

"Fine, let's bet. If you can't persuade me, then you buy me dinner," I said.

"That is a possibility. But why can't the CEO buy dinner?" he asked.

"Look here, this took me a month, and this just took you a day."

"The long and short of it must be measured to know." He did not bend.

"Let's not waste words. Let's go," I said.

We all left my office and went into the courtyard, where the garden was located. A few executives accompanied me. The auditor, who was trailing me, suddenly overtook me and walked with purpose towards where the rod was located. As soon as he saw me approach, he took a few steps back towards me.

"Mr. President, please pretend that you are about to take my picture and pose from that location."

"My, my, what strange things are happening today? I guess I will toast to myself in triumph tonight," I thought. I did as he said, and stood in front of him. I even posed as if I were holding a camera.

"Mr. President, do you see something?"

"I see you. You are a handsome fellow."

"No, not me. But something else."

"You're the only one there. What do you mean?" I grew annoyed.

"How can you not see it? You can't see it?"

"What do you mean? Are you teasing me?"

"Don't look at me, but look at what is behind me. Are you still blind to it?"

Oh heavens! Behind him, there were billboards advertising "Beef Broth Soup" and a neighborhood real estate office. It's right across from us, from a narrow road. The auditor smiles gleefully. An "I gotcha" look is on his face.

They insisted on going to the top-tier restaurant for dinner. The toast in celebration was made by Dr. Park. Other executives who were with us drank together. They joked that drinking with the boss tastes better.

"Don't look at the clouds, but the sun above," is one of my mantras, and yet I couldn't see the cheap looking signs advertising other wares right behind my shoulder. I was ashamed of myself.

"President Park, when our employees stand to take a picture by the 'face of KEPCO,' the background will no longer be ruined."

I wilted like a flower, as he snapped these words at me.

Time Waits for No One

We had about a year's worth of construction left for our new KEPCO headquarters. The chief architect came to me with a bunch of papers in his hand. He was trying to figure out where all the different departments should go. I looked at them, and they seemed all right to me, for the most part. But I looked at the parking lot's blueprint, and paused. It was only able to accommodate 250 cars.

"Why only 250?" I asked. I thought this would be a problem.

The architect argued that it would be more than enough. And even better, it would comply by construction standards of the day. I am somewhat bothered by this.

"Well. How many full-time employees will work at these offices?"

"About 3,000, [I believe]."

"Then it means that it won't even be able to house 10 percent of employees' cars."

"Why would this be a problem? We're doing this by the law."

"The law's not the problem. The era of "My Car" is upon us soon, and you think this is OK?"

"There is no problem. Why would employees need cars?"

"Oh really. Then double it to 500 parking slots."

Silence. He stares down at me. He doesn't want to comply.

"I said, increase it to 500."

He picks up all his papers and hurries out, with an annoyed look on his face.

Two years later, a few days after we all moved into the new offices, the architect came looking for me.

"There are not enough parking spaces for the employees."

The world is changing faster than we would like to admit.

The last part of construction was assigned to Kim Jae-sup, the chief architect. He was a man of no mistakes. Whenever I chanced upon him, he was always neat, even with all the "mess" around him. I know that it's hard to stay tidy, especially on a construction site because I've been there myself, in the Middle East. There is one thing common in construction sites that function smoothly, which is that the sites are organized and tidy.

He was an honor graduate of Seoul National University with an Engineering degree; he had also graduated from Daegu Technical High School, as I had. I once tried to promote him, but he respectfully declined. He said that this would show favoritism and cronyism, and only depress the morale of the other employees. He was a gentleman, through and through. I was deeply moved by this act.

But when I think back upon it, he should have been promoted. Why? Because of his humility. I really messed things up, haven't I, I thought to myself. Because of our friendship, I wanted him to do well. Dear Kim Jae-sup, I salute you.

After I had lost to auditor Park, I kept on thinking about the local real estate office and the beef broth soup shop. Nowadays, the neighborhood has undergone gentrification and the area is mostly clean, but even back then in the 1980s, it was not a "smart" place. We had to push for gentrification; otherwise, our new business offices there would suffer from a lack of prestige.

I couldn't take it. I wanted to come up with a solution. I kept thinking and thinking and finally realized that maybe I could build the KEPCO Art Center (now just a concert hall) there. Perhaps I could buy the land from them? That would be the best possible solution. I decided to go ahead with this plan.

The KEPCO Art Center concert hall was a long-cherished wish of mine. This would be a place where culture would merge with symposiums and science. I wanted it to house an electricity hall, science hall, culture hall, concert hall, an opera house, and be a multiplex for all. This place was supposed to nurture young minds towards developing an interest in electricity and science, and for the residents of Seoul, bring the convenience of a multiplex with cultural inclinations. In other words, I wanted to recreate a cradle of civilization, but within the spectrum of electric power.

Across the road, where the shops once stood, we planned to build the KEPCO Art Center after buying up all the land. I told the chief of public affairs, Park Won-tae, my thoughts about this project. I told him to keep it a secret, even while the project was being undertaken.

Park was a man of loyalty. He was a most popular man amongst his peers and his subordinates. Like they say in Korean, the "*Yaksayeoraebul*," for the "Buddha, the Physician of Souls," he was a beacon of light and everyone followed his lead. He was also a man who knew how to get things done.

We started with a basic investigation. The land we were about to purchase was about 10,000 *pyeong*, or over 30,000 m^2. The first problem was that many lay claims to this land. There were at least 32 land's owners in the area. If KEPCO wanted to buy the land, then the land's owners were sure to come swinging at us with their fists. If they collaborated, then the price of the land would skyrocket. We had to approach them cautiously. KEPCO could not actually say we were behind this plan.

That is why we decided to collaborate with Korean Air and push ahead with this project. This is what the former Chairman and CEO Cho Joong-Hoon, wanted while he was still living. Cho had come to me several times, asking me to sell Hanil General Hospital to him. We made a plan to have Korean Air buy the land, then exchange it with Hanil General Hospital. This would be good for the older sister, and good for the brother-in-law, as they say in Korean.

I hastily went to chairman and CEO Cho. At my request, he could not hide his happiness. He told me to stay put. He was over the moon.

"I will tell them to do the work, so you just stand and watch," he said.

It was secret and it seemed as though the work was going well. At first, it was smooth sailing. But from then onwards, the work didn't go so smoothly. Land speculation. The secret was out. It eludes me why and how, but even the information that the buyer was KEPCO, not the Korean Air (KAL) was leaked as well. To keep a secret safe is difficult no matter which era you're in. The price of the land kept on skyrocketing. There was no room for negotiations. Eventually, it was hard for us to stay in business, so to speak. We couldn't go ahead with our plans. Should we retreat? But we were so close. Give up? This was a word I did not wish to use. But I was pushed close to the ledge. I am still saddened by this. This also angered me. I couldn't fault anyone, so the situation made me even angrier. I was reminded of the common lesson that a deal should be done on one-on-one basis. I swallowed my tears and retreated. This turned out to be one and only task that I could not achieve during my tenure.

Heaven and Nature, and the Laws That Bind Them

The motto of the U.S. Army Inspector General (Army IG), this oath that they forever swear, paraphrased and translated from the Korean: "While working together for a cause, we must work with the bravery of a lion, two, with the loving hands of Lady Fortuna, and three, investigate with the sharp claws of an Eagle."

After I finished my term as the CEO of KEPCO, the Board of Audit and Inspection of Korea investigated my comings and goings during my entirety of my career there, for a period of three months. If they had searched for that long, then they would have found a lot of bad things. Well, they would have found some nuggets of gold there too. To investigate does not always mean that they are on the hunt for blood. They also look at whether a prize should be awarded, if any. Doesn't the Army IG also talk about loving hands? There were no harsh words of censure directed at me, but no praise either.

Let's take KEPCO, for example. We investigate what employees did wrong, but we also point out what employees did right. It's an additional point system. Effort outweighs failure. We evaluate the performances. Apathy cannot hide here. Who did the most amount of work? When this question is asked, what kind of honest person doesn't want to raise his hand?

A society afraid of failure is a society without a future.

Why do we pursue public service? It is nothing more than a sense of duty to make a world where logic and rule of law prevail!

The scholars and the leaders are inept. Logic has closed its eyes, and the Righteous have hidden their whereabouts. I do not have the right to say this, myself. But because we all live in this society together, let us all pause and worry for a moment.

Today's society almost makes it impossible to survive. Whose fault is this? Is it partly to do with the intellectuals, or the public officials, or the leaders, shunning the reason and rationality? It is because it puts profit before the public good. It is because it loses its way.

"When the woman saw that the fruit of the tree was good for food and pleasing to the eye, and also desirable for gaining wisdom, she took some and ate it. She also gave some to her husband, who was with her, and he ate it" (Genesis 3:6), New International Version.

Desire is at the root of all evils, even from the very beginnings of mankind's history; this is detailed in the Book of Genesis. This is embedded in our DNA.

Yes, this is Man. Most people are like this. Then what is the difference between a public official and a man of humble origins who isn't weighed down by responsibility?

Life knocks down the public official, the same as any other man; this is what the laws of Nature dictate nowadays. Be the recipient of cronyism and still play with the rest? That isn't fair. You have to shrug off your titles or feel the weight of them and act like a man appointed to public office.

Those who serve the public are not your usual run-of-the-mill type. They have to have a sense of the elite who enjoy privileges that aren't usually available to other members of society: the bourgeoisie, if you will. However, you need to temper this sense of privilege with a spirit of service and sacrifice. This does not refer to always giving in, for example: "This body will die, and die, a hundred times over, without change." A sense of duty must always follow a purpose. This is duty in action. A public official, no matter how lowly his status on the pecking ladder, must always be imbued with at least a small measure of duty.

This world always has truths as well as lies. But the leaders utter lies disguised as truths without even battling an eye. I do not wish to debate "*In Eui Yae Ji*," or the four characteristics that define Man; these characteristics include benevolence, righteousness, propriety, and wisdom. Even a father who has nothing to be proud of should be able to save his face before his sons. But these leaders were not ashamed of ruining their dignity before their own people. What were they thinking?

In this world of today, you trust people less and less. Woe to today's world, because this loss of faith is detrimental to society. Nowadays, it's "do what you wish"; aside from the inherent selfishness in this type of thinking, this newish dogma will shake our society to its very foundations.

Lao-Tzu says, "Man takes his law from the Earth; the Earth takes its law from Heaven; and Heaven takes its law from the Tao." This may sound old-fashioned to you. But every culture that upholds truth speaks of "an individual man's duty and Heaven's will" in some form or another. When these truths and transcendental values are not highly esteemed, a catastrophe occurs.

A person's duty is within his reach. He inherits the Earth. He reaps what he sows. For example, when you plant beans, you get beans, and when you plant red beans, you get red beans; this is the law of Nature. Be honest, then success will follow, and endure, then success will also follow. If you endure, then you abide by the law. Withstanding all, including great sorrows and great pain, is possible when you put your mind to it; anyone is capable of this.

"And in the morning, 'Today it will be stormy, for the sky is red and overcast.' You know how to interpret the appearance of the sky, but you cannot interpret the signs of the times." (Matthew 16:3, New International Version)

Just because you cannot see the sun, doesn't mean that the sun isn't there. Only searching for the harmonious, yet hidden dictates of Heaven, while remaining blind to the symbol of the times, means that we are a nation without hope.

The Pursuit of the Beauty

I said too many harsh things. Let me talk of something more pleasant. About 50 to 60 years ago, there was a Japanese mathematician named Oka Kiyoshi (1901–1978). He was a promising young scholar, so he obtained the means to study abroad in France. Three years in, and he still hadn't produced a thesis. He went to an older alumnus and said that upon returning to Japan, he would investigate Basho's haikus. "Haiku" is a traditional type of Japanese poetry and "Basho" is the father of the haiku. That a mathematician should become a haiku specialist! The alumnus, who was speechless, said to him:

"What do you mean, [study] haikus?"

"After studying in France, I realized that while these peoples' culture is high indeed, our traditional Japanese culture is even more venerable."

"So?"

"I want to learn our ways, our culture. And by that, I mean the haiku."

The apex of the conversation came to a head; in Korean, we call this "*jeomip gakyung*."

"My dear fellow, do be reasonable."

He is met with silence. He doesn't even respond.

A few years pass, and Oka returns to Osaka. He still hasn't written his thesis.

But upon his return, he really becomes a pupil of "Basho" and puts in his all at haikus. Everyone around him is astonished. That such a promising scholar with his whole future ahead of him was doing something that they considered foolhardy.

Some time passed, as it always does. Then the mathematics world was astounded by the publication and presentation of a thesis. Oka had solved a difficult problem, with three parts, that involved several variable analyses. He achieved this in 1935. He had done this on his own. The entire world, not to mention Japan, was shocked.

He was fastidious and notoriously bad-tempered. Every day, during the research phase, he would check his mental state. He would leave a plus sign or a minus sign next to each date, depending on his mood. On plus days, he would work, but on minus days, he would not even rise and would only sleep.

His methodology towards work was this: "As you plant a seed and wait, it will take some time for it to germinate and bear fruit. As such, research involves the similar methodology of patience. If you do all this with sincerity, then even a seed that has fallen to the bottom of your consciousness will germinate, sprout from the hard ground and see the light of day."

In the mathematics world, there is a prize that is coveted almost as much, or even more than the Nobel Prize. It is called the Fields Medal. A Canadian mathematician called John Fields established this in 1936. The prize was monetary, about $15,000 CAD. It is only awarded to those under the age of 40, making this even more difficult to win than the Nobel Prize, according to world pundits.

In 2014, the International Mathematics Union held its international congress at Starfield COEX Mall, in southern Seoul. More than 5,000 scholars from over 100 countries gathered to debate the world's hardest mathematical problems and present their theses.

At this event, the Fields Medal was awarded. Oka did not win a medal, but his compatriots in Japan have, to date, earned three. We have to play catch up. In many fields, Japan is ahead of us by about 50 years.

Let us change the subject and return to the problematic Oka. He was invited by the Japanese imperial family to visit them. The emperor was proud of him and asked him:

"How do you good at mathematics?"

Everyone assembled there waited with bated breath, and stared at the mathematician's lips.

"Your venerable majesty, it has to do with chasing that ideal, beauty."

What did he mean by this? At his slightly absurdist response, everyone cocked their heads.

"I see!" This is what the emperor said.

The Japanese revere their Emperor like a god. Who would open their mouths next? Everyone's heads are bowed.

A special guest, a journalist, appeared frustrated with Oka's simple yet elegant answer. But he could not just ask a question or make a remark in front of the Emperor himself!

That is why several days later, he visited Professor Oka.

"Dear Professor, what did you mean that day at the imperial palace?"

"Math is Beauty."

"What do you mean?"

"Ahem, I already said it."

Again, silence in a vacuum.

"What a stubborn fellow," the journalist thought to himself. He started getting cantankerous.

"What do you mean?"

"Math is beauty itself, is what I mean."

The journalist's curiosity gets the best of him. To say that mathematics is beauty itself, when it personally gives him such a headache.

"Can you stop talking in riddles and tell me what you mean?"

"Well, mathematics' true nature is beauty itself. That is why in order to do well in math, you must chase that elusive ideal, beauty."

The journalist felt like he may have understood, but he is still at a loss for words. He is confused. Is this why Oka set such store by "haikus"? But what is the correlation between haikus and mathematics?

In school, there is a firm divide between the humanities and the sciences; the two remain apart in separate worlds. I myself find math gives me a headache, and found myself embracing the humanities instead. Well, I must say. I find myself stuck between understanding and not understanding. I am confused.

There is a phrase in Korean called, "*jeonilseong*." To put it simply, everything in the universe is interconnected. It seems as though we are living in separate worlds, but it's similar to the Westerners' belief in the "Butterfly Effect."

Between you and me, Einstein's theory of the space-time continuum is another example of "*jeonilseong*," in my opinion. To the average person, space and time remain separate; and yet, in the fourth dimension, they appear to be interconnected. Even the theoretical physicist David Bohm, a Nobel Prize winner, says that consciousness and material things start from the same place, then diverge by transforming into a different type of substance. Isn't the universe grand? The universe started with the first words in the Good Book, then there is "*do*," or a moral code of conduct, then Beauty, then Truth. All these things we hold to be true, that they all start from the same place.

Current physicists have shed light on the truthfulness of the universe, but in the East, we have already known this. Hence, in Buddhism we have "the nature of Buddha," then the absoluteness of truth, and in Hinduism, we have the "supreme principle of the universe," and Lao Tzu spoke often of "*Hyundong*."

When the grand universe is like this, then how can the humanities and the sciences be different from each other, and how could we say that mathematics and haikus are not interrelated?

And so it follows that the absolute truth becomes as one, then Oka's admission that the pursuit of that ideal, Beauty, can be a way to approach mathematics. He is correct, a hundred times over.

When we analyze Picasso's paintings, then it disintegrates into a few paints and chemical substances. Beethoven's beautiful symphonies can be distilled into high or low air pressure and vibrations. How could a few paints become art, and how could the vibrations in the air become Beethoven's beautiful symphonies, the very classics of music?

This is because of the beauty of heaven and nature. It is infused with the soul, and it has life. You can even call this the absolute truth of "*do*," or beauty that permeates through the universe. The universe, during its very beginnings, became infused with a purpose when God blew his breath and gave birth to Life.

So it is established that when one behaves in accordance with the great principles, the universe itself is governed by the principles of Beauty and Truth, and understanding these will contribute to an even greater Good.

The universe is accurate, right and true.

To be human, what does this mean?

Disregarding the three principles I have mentioned above, it may be that there is a drive towards an insatiable curiosity, a thirst for pleasures of the flesh as well as the mind, and a proclivity towards Bacchanalian pleasures whenever the opportunity presents itself. At every opportunity, trying to own, or take over, or show off. These are all fine. Because these qualities are only too human.

But at the same time, many people do not lose their curiosity over what is beautiful, what is pure, and what is true. These are all beautiful qualities.

The curious thing is, an all too benevolent God accepts all these dichotomies. Isn't this strange? Shouldn't He have suppressed our more carnal desires? But to us humans, he has given us the gift of free will, along with all that is Good, True, and Pure. To mere animals, he has not granted them this type of freedom.

How great is this love! He shows us the depth of His benevolence. So it follows that we have to examine the deep meaning behind His will. This applies especially towards those involved in government or public affairs. A public official walks the tightrope between receiving kickbacks and earning respect. This important title is married to a government salary. How frightening yet great is this seat of power? The title of a government official is married to a frightening amount of responsibility and duty. But a few (foolhardy) men say they will play with the rest instead of taking up the mantle of duty. How shameless of them! How one shudders for them on their Day of Judgment! How weighty is the responsibility that they bear!

Those who say God is dead at least have some charm. They are brave. But how afraid must they have been to say such a thing? That they deny the existence of God is a rather strong type of a belief that Westerners call atheism.

They do not have the power to deny yet come up with excuses and wrap lies around something and call it Good? They are the ones who are truly lost, those who are ruthlessly cold-blooded. The worst of these fellows, in my humble opinion? They are the pro-North leftists. How can they set such store by the father, son, and grandson that started with Kim Il-Sung? The North Korean regime is one that is shrouded in hypocrisy. We know this, and yet, refuse to deny outright. This is pure cowardice. They try to overthrow the Republic of Korea's government. If they really have a conscience, then they should help their own, who are suffering injustices that go against the very principles of humanity. They are the hypocrites that rule their land and brethren, to this very day.

To those leaders in public office, great or small, I would like to raise a question. The universe starts with the "Word," then all that is Good, and True, and Pure. How can they continue with their lies and hypocrisy? What happened to their activism for the "voice of [our mutual conscience]," and "the shouts of righteousness?" Why have they thrown these away?

CHAPTER 12

Enertopia

Restoring Vision

In August 1983, I paid a visit to Taiwan, ahead of my participation in the American Nuclear Society, or ANS's, annual conference. At the time, the chief of the nuclear power plant at Kori, Lee Jong-hun, accompanied me. He is the one who planted in me a vision of an "Enertopia."

It was the first year of my appointment as chief operating officer of KEPCO, so this was when I was trying to envision a future for the Korea Electric Power Corporation. During this time, Lee helped me with the scientific knowledge as well as assuaging the prejudices I may have had during this time against nuclear power. I became a proponent of nuclear power myself, after listening to him speak many times. I believed that until this point, an energy efficient society, or "Enertopia," had been impossible, but now made possible through nuclear energy. We were able to reestablish BWRs, or boiling water reactors, and completely quell the issue of its adoption through Lee. It also meant technologically, we could remain independent from this point forward.

The Fukushima Daiichi Power Plant also employs BWRs. Japan has changed its models to heavy water reactors, instead of light water reactors. This shows how advanced the Republic of Korea's nuclear power industry is; it is top-notch. My trip to Japan was about three nights and four days. I learned a lot about nuclear energy during this particular business trip.

What surprised me the most was the ability to reuse nuclear fuel. To me, it seemed like a dream. I couldn't believe it. Then it could reduce its reliance on oil and coal and the national energy production would then rely heavily on nuclear power. At the time of this writing, we still import uranium, but from a certain point, theoretically-speaking, we could reuse the byproducts once we had enough piled up. There was no better goblin's bat (a Korean euphemism to imply that anything is possible).

North Korea has reserves of uranium, some of the most in the world. When reunification happens, then there will be no need to import uranium. The problem is nuclear energy technology. True technological independence is only possible when we do not have to import uranium. True nuclear technology independence will turn the Korean peninsula from an energy-impoverished state to an energy-rich state; freeing us from the bondage of energy dependence. Enertopia starts from technology independence. The way forward was clear.

But there was one concern. That was that of safety. As a former active battalion commander in the army, I have been part of the Nuclear Support Team, or NST, many times. NST also involves the launching of nuclear warheads. I know the danger of nuclear power and nuclear yield all too well. It is still a frightening thought, what may happen if it falls into the wrong hands.

Lee introduced me to Dr. Milton Levenson at the annual ANS meeting. Levenson was the then-president of the American Nuclear Society and a formidable expert in the field of nuclear energy (he passed away in 2018). Lee wanted me to understand from the perspective of a person who had decades of experience in nuclear energy research. This was his foresight in action.

"Mr. Park, I am a person who has participated, from the very beginning, in the Eisenhower scheme of 'Atoms for Peace.' If you are worried about nuclear energy then I wish to say just one thing. For example..."

It appeared as though he was puzzling over how to explain this to an amateur. He started with another example.

"Let's say that we toss this book from the rooftop of this building. Most likely, the book will fall. This is gravity in action. But the book can also spike up. This is likely due to a strong gust of wind. When I was a participant in the very early phases of bringing nuclear energy into fruition, the safety of nuclear power took into account radical, even unforeseen changes."

I did not have any further questions.

A man who is born and lives in a particular time is tasked with a small act, a personal duty, if you will. This is fate, and also *Cheonmyung* (a mandate from Heaven) in action. This may be hidden from plain view. Or you may know, but miss it anyway. But the Heavens always demand answers. If you are only looking out for your selfish personal interests, then the nation may topple. All these things come from everyone disregarding the *Cheonmyung* during one generation or another.

With all due respect, I do not believe in the Marxist historical theory. In my humble opinion, I believe history is the complex interplay and outcome of human relationships. Our free will influences the whole of human history.

As for me on a personal level, achieving KEPCO's technology independence was more similar to the Western concept of take it or leave it. But had I taken this route, what would have happened? We would have not had a good power supply, and because of rising energy costs, our competitive edge in business would have suffered, and we would not be enjoying the fruits of our economic prosperity today. That is why everyone has a task, and whilst working, there are rules to follow. Whether one knows this, doesn't know it, does it, or doesn't do it, the rise and fall of the person and the organization depends upon it.

From my appointment as CEO of KEPCO, I have borne witness to the call, as well as the conscience, of the times. If our ancestors a hundred years ago had had this type of knowledge, then we would not have endured tragedy in the years to follow.

When you look back upon it, the most important part is "timing." Even if you are aware of something, if you miss the timing, then everything goes amiss. This is the real world. You must not miss the timing.

I am the CEO of KEPCO. Why am I here? How long do I have? Not everything can go according to my will. Sometimes I move. Sometimes I miss the timing. Technological independence is better the faster it is achieved. Let's start now.

Some may say that if the drive for technology independence that we strove for in the early 1980's hadn't happened, we would have failed after all. The Chernobyl disaster and the Three Mile Island incident, also known as the TMI accident, caused many to shy away from anything nuclear for a while.

But we made good use of this gap in the market, and this was the key to our success. When everyone said that this was a dead market, and gave up, we continued. That is why success is so mysterious; the timing must be right. This is what Confucius called, "*Shijoong*," or a proper timing.

Our long march commenced.

Lim Han-que, Chief of the Division

Once in a thousand, or so the saying goes in Korean, and we were ordered to make nuclear power plants 11th and 12th (otherwise known as Younggwang 3 and 4), technologically independent of other countries. We decided to increase our new business venture arm and appointed Lim Han-que to head this division. But we did not increase the number of employees in this division. Below him were only five employees, starting with Chung Geon, who was in charge of contracts. He was a graduate of Seoul National University's (SNU) law program and a man of superior talents. Han Guk-jong, who had gone to SNU's business program, was his direct subordinate. He would eventually become KEPCO's vice president. Then Lee Joong-jae, who had graduated from Seoul National University's Engineering school, and one of the top KEPCO employees who knew a lot about Nuclear Engineering. Then Kim Jong-shin, who would eventually become the CEO of the Korea Hydro and Nuclear Power Co., Ltd. (KHNP), another subsidiary of KEPCO. This all took place in June of 1984.

Everyone was so surprised. The important point was that the human resources division had picked such unexpected candidates for this branch. This is because even KEPCO by this point had so many qualified, world-class candidates such as Goh Joong-myung, Lee Chang-geon, Suh Seok-cheon, Noh Yun-rae, Lee Ho-rim, Choi Jang-dong, Chun Jae-poong, Hong Joo-bo, Lee Joong-jae, etc.

But to ignore the bright luminaries and pick Lim Han-que instead! A minority! What else could they expect from a CEO who knew so little about nuclear power (or so they thought). There were concerns from the get-go from even the friendly, interested parties.

I had taken a lot of thought into helping HR pick these men. We had too many men, rather than too few men. The best part of it was that in our nation's (modern) history, nuclear power was about just as long. By the time we were able to prepare building the 11th and 12th nuclear power plants, we had already been operating three nuclear power plants. We were also in the process of building seven. But out of the ones in operation and the ones still in development, all were Westinghouse and Bechtel's, with the exception of those located in Uljin. They had built and were still operating the Kori Nuclear Reactor 1, and about ten years after the initial construction, must have seen and heard just about everything there was to know about nuclear power. There must have been "*jeong*" between them too, both good and bad.

In order for technology independence to be achieved, you must remain impartial from other stresses, such as petty politics. You also have to be cold-hearted sometimes, even forgoing friendship and long-standing ties. This is not because you do not trust them. It is because friendship and long-standing friendships sometimes can be problematic. But throughout life, you have to foster relationships. That is why for ten years, those who had a relationship with the Westinghouse model, to put those very men in charge, seemed cruel. That is why I worried for several days, and for several days more.

They said, you must put in charge those without relationships that bind, or those that have never seen the bright lights of Vegas. They had to be stubborn, working quietly on the fringes, inflexible, and not influential.

Lim Han-que. He and I had some bad blood between us. During my tenure at the Korea Heavy Industries (now Doosan Enerbility), I had tried to merge it with KEPCO's construction arm. This is when Lim voiced his first complaints, adamantly, at that. "Well what have we here, the world is an unknowable mystery. I cannot believe that he's actually here as the new CEO," he must have thought to himself. The taste in his mouth must have been bitter. He must have wanted to avoid running into me. "But what is this! To be promoted as the head of the new business ventures division?" But I liked his stubbornness, to be honest. One day, I called on Lim to dine with me. At a quiet, well-lighted place. It was supposed to be just us.

"Mr. Lim! We can do great things together. I have great faith in you."

I did not need to say more. I just told him exactly what he needed to know, but was sparse with details.

The most important quality of the new team was to ensure fairness and secrecy. To that end, it was to run as an independent unit that does not allow anyone's interference. Even a CEO was not an exception. Another "Need to Know" principle was to be applied, which was a basic principle to run an intelligence agency. It means that "only someone who needs to know" will know.

When the new "class" of recruits began their work, I called the team, and in addition, a higher level executive, Lee Won-bae, along with Chung

Geon, and Lee Joong-jae, and said this to them:

"We have now started this historic undertaking of nuclear technology independence. I want to stress just one thing. It is in your own hands to select who will be the one to take care of the 11th and the 12th nuclear power reactors. It is neither up to a minister nor up to the CEO. Therefore, I sincerely hope that you will follow your hearts as engineers, to choose the best possible option."

Everyone stared at the floor. They must have been happy with their new line of work, yet were still worried and perplexed. But as soon as I finished speaking, they all looked up at me then at each other. What? To decide for themselves? Was this really possible? Everyone seemed to doubt his own ears. Oh no. This new CEO is too green; he really doesn't have the slightest inkling. It's been about ten years for them working in the field of nuclear energy, and yet, the CEO's decision-making power was now in their own hands.

"The responsibility lies with us now. We can't believe it. But this is what the CEO says with a serious face. And we can't ask any more questions," they must have thought.

A heavy silence followed.

"I understand what you mean. We will have ourselves prepared."

Lim says this in a low voice. And so this awkward meeting came to an end.

The Loser's Bitter Cup of Defeat

It must have been September 1984. Han Guk-jong, another head of yet another department, comes in with some official documents in his hand. It must have been regarding foreign capital management. Han Guk-jong, an outstanding man of talent with a degree from Seoul National University. His name was impressive, and his character, impeccable. I nicknamed him "Mr. Korea."

"What is this?"

"Well..."

With a worried look, he hands over the documents. It is the Architect-Engineering contract with Bechtel. Bechtel had built the Kori 3 and Kori 4 reactors.

"Well...I mean to say...that it is Bechtel's contract, but the payment date is fast approaching."

"If it is a contract, then we can just pay for it, can't we?"

"Well...we have a slight problem," he said.

"What do you mean, a slight problem?" I asked.

"Well…the explanation is a bit long…"

With a trembling voice, he started explaining why he was so worried, and I started doubting my own ears. To be brief, when the contract was first drawn up, it was $80,000, but because of increasing man-hours,• it now amounted to $120 million. That it would jump by this much! I began calculating in my head. Even if the original contract favored Bechtel, a 10 percent increase was reasonable, but a 50 percent price increase made no sense. I slammed my fist onto the table.

I remembered my years in the Middle East, where I had signed similar contracts. I had even overseen the building of structures in the same area. For construction work, there is an organization that governs the contracts all over the world: this is called the International Federation of Consulting Engineers, or FIDIC. FIDIC contracts are supposed to protect both parties. In the event that there may be unforeseen charges, it ensures a price ceiling. This rule applies unless the construction work is something like weapons development or spacecraft, where costs may not be so easily estimated.

In case of Bechtel, it was just nothing but personnel expenses, but the number, which was a rise of 50 percent in deposit, was outrageous. This is just unacceptable! This anger should have been faced by the person who made the deal or the executive in charge, but this messenger had to face it. I was sorry, but the counterpart was Mr. Han. Nobody else.

"I cannot, and will not pay!" I declined to authorize the payment. Han became flustered, then left my office.

I called all those who had been involved in the contract to my office. They are full of excuses. The contract was viable. It was also customary, ac-

• The amount of work done by one person in one hour.

cording to them. They are explaining the inexplicable to me, and they were pretty good. But I am still very angry. I was displeased with the situation, and all the explanations made my blood boil.

During the course of the conversation, one person piped up.

"This is a contract. It is the be-all and end-all. It is a contract that our company, KEPCO, has to abide by as it is an international contract."

This comment made me erupt.

"What? An international contract? You call this a contract? I want the contract deemed null and void, and will not pay."

I uttered a few curses.

All the employees assembled in my office turned pale with surprise. That the contract would be destroyed! This was an entirely new ball game. This tsunami made no sense. Was the CEO Ebenezer Scrooge instead of Father Christmas? Maybe I went a bit too far.

"I cannot and will not pay! Leave me!" I shouted at them.

The very next day, vice president Mun Hee-seong came in with the papers. From bourgeoisie roots, and a graduate of the famous Kyunggi High School, located in Gangnam, southern Seoul, he was the type who would have succeeded, with flying colors, in any discipline.

Vice president Lee Jong-hun told me about Mun below:

While still at Seoul National University, a professor wrote a math problem on the chalkboard. It was a test to see the level of expertise (or lack thereof) of the new freshmen. But alas! Most of them were staring at each other, without approaching the chalkboard. And then from amidst the crowd, emerged a very handsome fellow, who started solving the problem. The rest of the classroom seemed restless and nervous. Then the student returned to his seat. With respectful eyes, the professor gazed at the student.

"What is your name?"

"Mun Hee-seong, sir."

And now, returning to the issue at hand:

The department in charge of the contract must have had a headache from my temper tantrum from the previous day. Someone was bound to get hurt. But that problem had to be dealt with later. So what was the most pressing issue? They had to assuage the hurt and angry feelings of the CEO, who wanted the contract terminated. Terminate the contract? In the business world, this would be an unprecedented move. This was a contract agreed upon by Bechtel. What kind of company was Bechtel? At the time, it had over 200,000 employees and it was one of the largest privately owned corporations in the United States. It was the rare company that would be passed down through generations of a single bloodline. During this time period, George Schultz, the Secretary of State, was from this company, as well as the Secretary of Defense, Caspar W. Weinberger. To terminate a contract with such an illustrious company?

The department in charge of contracts must have tried to come up with a solution on its own, by even working throughout the night. It was clear that it was frightened of the CEO and frightened of Bechtel. What a dilemma. Who would wear the corona of myrtle? Their way forward must have been like walking through a dark tunnel. The last possible resort was to use a shield. A human one by the name of Vice President Mun. They must have been clinging onto him, begging for mercy. Mun probably wasn't very happy about this. "Why should I?" he would have thought. But he couldn't refuse to not help. That is why he was a great man, a true giant amongst men.

The following day, vice president Mun came into my office.

"What brings you here?" I looked at him coolly.

"I..." A smile crosses his face. He's suddenly turned into a beatific Buddha.

"I will solve this problem myself."

"Ok! See yourself out."

I had nothing to complain about. He's the king's man. I just need to observe him. Let's see how well he does. He has connections, both here and abroad. He must have connections at Bechtel too. If I could agree to the new conditions, then I would sign and pay.

I waited and waited. For a very long time. I didn't hear much about what was happening. I had predicted this, somewhat, anyway. Bechtel's holier than thou attitude would not be easily bent. Amongst the employees, there must have been chaos. As a contract that had seen the light of day by following FIDIC guidelines, we could not just declare it null and void; it had already been signed by the prior parties. Bechtel could have sued us. And as Bechtel got more stubborn, the CEO of KEPCO wasn't budging. Without a solution in sight, he was just refusing. The king's man must have felt awful too, stuck between a rock and a hard place.

Now everyone became too nervous to make a full report. Everyone was trapped between Bechtel and the CEO of KEPCO. There was no exit. They were shrouded in darkness.

A long time passed. We received news from Bechtel. The owner, Bechtel Jr., would visit South Korea. Ok, I thought. Now the negotiations would begin. I waited. But the date of their arrival passed, without any more news. We asked around. The biggest surprise? They had already visited and left. They hadn't even visited KEPCO. They had only visited the Blue House. My God, they had totally disrespected me. It was like a slap in the face.

His message was clear. "Mr. Park, be careful. You should pick your fights carefully. You have disturbed a sleeping giant."

But I refused to give up. Yes, we were losing. The other side was brandishing a sword. From the onset, it appeared as though I was the perpetrator of the fight, and Bechtel was right, a thousand times over. To renegotiate, to draw up a new contract, or declare the old one invalid, was just too much. That's the way it was. But I wanted to discuss sound business ethics, before honoring the terms of the contract. Does this make sense? Because it made no sense to me. That $80 million could, in a year, become $120 million. The next year, it would jump to $200 million, then who would stop it when it ballooned into over $300 million?

Sometimes, sheer brawn wins over everything else. This is a bitter cup to swallow. Let us toast to the weak.

So I drank from the bitter cup. Sheer strength and justification were within the fist of the giant; what else could I do? Across the Pacific Ocean, somewhere, they were drinking champagne (or so I imagined).

But to sign the unfair contract, and approve it, was too much of a bitter pill to swallow. For about 10 days, I kept my silence. Employees on both sides of the Pacific were in a bind. Even from the other side, they had used their brains (and their brawn), and must have been surprised at my resistance. They were also frustrated. But I kept my silent disapproval. This was unheard of. This was I, acting without a script, without sound countermeasures in sight.

Bechtel was fidgeting and fretting over my resistance. I requested a meeting with Mr. Reinsch, the President of Engineering at the Bechtel Corporation. I said I would sign, but before, I had some things to say. This actually was me trying to buy some more time. It must have been Director

Han Guk-jong who gave me a tip. He remained true to his reputation as a man of authority in contract management, by telling me that if we check every single slip on the "man hour" clauses on that side. It was his theory that there must be something, and we could find it if we check every single detail, and he suggested that we do this in that very year's regular audit.

Via God's grace, or what we say in the East, "*cheonwoo shinjo*," it was obvious that from the drawing up of the contract, the ball was in Bechtel's court, so to speak. That is why the annual inspections were just a perfunctory measure, without any real merit. But this time, we would assemble a real inspection team. So from our end, we had to pick employees who spoke English well enough to communicate with the other team, and add more accounting specialists, and train all of them well.

Bechtel accepted my request. In generous gesture, Mr. Reinsch himself would visit me. All right, I thought to myself. Between his comings and goings, we would be able to buy even more time.

So finally, the Bechtel President Reinsch came. He was visibly proud and triumphant. After all, he was here to accept surrender. I treated him in a respectful manner, with hospitality. I spent time with him, one-on-one, without the rest of the team. My earnest requests and pleas were listened to at every turn.

"Imagine, for a minute, that you are in my shoes. How would you feel, taking into account all these [unfair clauses] in the contract?"

The cold-blooded nature of business became more human from here onwards. However, we were still at the "I will consider" stage. But I could not ask for more. This was enough. I had bought some time, and had a conversation with Bechtel's CEO, man-to-man.

Without the need for further discussion, I sent the audit team to the other side of the world. The one on whose shoulders rested an immense amount of responsibility was the head of the audit office at the time, Kim Myung-hwan. He was a graduate of the Seoul National University's Law School, and he was one of the best administrators I had then seen to date. Tall, with handsome good looks, he was what we call in Korean "*seonpoong dohgol*," or of a serene, yet ascetic nature. The team he assembled was the best of the best.

When they touched down in Los Angeles, after a long transcontinental flight, the audit team headed straight to the Bechtel headquarters. Bechtel appeared flummoxed; the Koreans were not heading straight to the hotel to unpack their bags and do a little sightseeing. Instead, we went straight to work.

The next day, we demanded to see paperwork. What about that one, and this one too, and it was really a sight to behold, from what I was told later. Yes, Bechtel did not know what my team was really up to, but we had free rein, for the time being. To Bechtel, it appeared as though we were really making a big fuss over nothing. But for the KEPCO team, it was different. We had spent two months preparing for this overseas business trip. If something went wrong, the men sent there could not return.

It must have been quite a sight for Bechtel, as we demanded documents that to them, seemed inconsequential, even foolish. But we were the very embodiment of "*seongdong kyuksuh*," or looking in one direction while secretly rowing in the opposite. This would assuage their fears, for the time being. What we were up to after all were slips that were used to calculate those "man hours." There must have been numbers involved to make those calculations. I mean, the number of hours that they calculate in their offices over the Pacific. There is no way that they were errors-free. And on the fifth day, the weak points started to rise. A dozen cases will be enough to be fatally damage Bechtel. It was an issue about honesty and honor. And these two are the virtues that Americans show zero tolerance. Errors started to be discovered, and there were several dozens. Inside my heart, I was crying with joy. I could finally show them verifiable data as proof and confronted them.

At this time, Bechtel must have become greatly startled, or "*daekyung shilsaek,*" or truly, turned pale with astonishment. They had totally seen us as weaklings, unable to put up resistance for a true fight. And yet, and the end, they had to tuck their tails behind their legs and agree with us. We Koreans, on our part, did not address them with severity. We simply requested a "ceiling," or cap on the original contract. Business is all about "give and take," remember?

Sometimes, even they have to drink from a bitter cup.

"I salute you, my astonishing audit team!"

Crossing the Bridge of No Return

While in this business of nuclear power, we Koreans have drunk too many bitter cups to swallow. During the past 10 or so years, from the perspective of the company to company operations, on sites, and even at a foreign engineer's quarters, we were sometimes humiliated beyond description for our ignorance.

Once, we had to reimburse a Bechtel engineer for his eyeglasses; he had dropped them in front of his quarters. These instances were all examples of unfair contracts. We cannot but blame ourselves for our foolishness and naiveté.

But I say to you now, that someone should summarize these anecdotes and lessons, at the very least. As they say in the East, "*washin sangdam*," perseverance through hard times can serve as a model for the younger generations that follow.

If it has been 10 years already, then it's time to stop being an indentured servant. It was time for us to learn technological independence. The Kori Nuclear Reactor 1 and 2 had the so-called "turnkey" contracts, but the

Kori 3 and 4, done with the initiative of our side as we divided the duties, still gave us no share of core technology. I mean, I knew that they were stingy with their technology, and there was no way that they would share them for free. But that was not the single problem here. Another problem was the lack of our own determination to get things done. So far, we have claimed that we have earned about 40 percent of the nuclear technology. It was good to hear. But there was no core technology. We were just toying with the BOP (Balance of Plant) and their periphery. We had to get to the root of the nuclear technology. It was about time.

To all my fellow men that work in nuclear engineering!

I say to you now, watch them. For the Nuclear Power Plants 11 and 12, we will achieve technological independence.

To all my KEPCO men!

Try harder! There are great tasks on the horizon for us.

As Confucius said, men of real virtue train their bodies in order to achieve greatness under the mandate of Heaven.

For the Nuclear Power Plants 11 and 12 (Younggwang Nuclear Power Plants 3 and 4), we finally had a new business team that ordered and evaluated nuclear power plants. In July 1984, KEPCO and its subsidiaries and partners created this new group. In order for us to learn and pass down this technology, we had to put their names down as the main contractors, as green as they were. If we all came together for this new mission, then it would ensure cooperation. It turns out the nuclear energy research institute's day to day operations might be put to the test, but with the help of the new group, it would not falter. The new group was composed of the following: Korea Heavy Industry and Construction (KHIC, or the Doosan Heavy Industries and Construction Co., Ltd. as it is now known), KEPCO Nuclear Fuel (former

Korea Nuclear Fuel Company, or KNFC), Korea Gas Corporation, Korea Electrical Safety Corporation, and the Institute of Atomic Energy Research, to name a few. The purpose of this new group, comprised of men from these companies, was to achieve technological independence in the near future.

In January 1985, under KEPCO executive Min Kyung-sik's watch, we started to work on the draft of ITB, which was a guide for bidding. We had always been in the position of students when it came to nuclear energy, but this time, we were trying to work on ITB, which was a challenging task for our teacher figures. It was beyond our capacity. Besides, we were trying to do that without help from outside, only within the KEPCO territory. There were many who worried for us. The foreign companies laughed at us; what would or did a Korean know? But Min's team outdid all our expectations. In November 1985, we sent the ITB to the bidding companies.

The foreign companies who had expected our folly and laughed at us were astonished. They were taken aback by how there were no mistakes in our work. First, we drew a clear line in the sand, by taking care of ambiguous details such as upkeep expenses, compensation, and security reassurances. We excluded them or made sure that there can be no way to make exceptions. Secondly, we had the compensation of design's service cost fixed and calculated in respective additions. This was to fix our weakness, which ended up giving us bitter cups of defeat to Bechtel. Thirdly, we specified 100% technology instructions, which was what we were hoping for.

As far as the other party, up to this point, they had kept their cool. But when the contract with the exception of technological specifications was to be written in Hangeul, the Korean alphabet created by King Sejong the Great, their lids blew off. France, to this day, is proud of their national language, and Framatome, which designs and operates nuclear power plants, sent a one-sided message, saying they were abandoning the project. We sent a message in response, saying: "We will not stop you."

For about a fortnight, they fretted, and then grudgingly accepted our terms; we accepted them gladly, without complaint.

The reason why I insisted on the contract being written mostly in Korean was because I had gotten the short end of the stick in the Middle East, way too many times to count. Every single word we fought over, over and over. I was proud to use Hangeul, designed by our national forefather, King Sejong the Great, to draw up the main contract. So I ended up wielding the sword, and nitpicking over the terms instead of the other way around. This made me immensely proud and cheerful.

For about 10 months, we commenced with our work; it was painstakingly done, and cut to the bone. A lot of vacation days were not used. There were days when we stayed up all night. This is because we KEPCO men did not outsource any of our work with contractors. The ones who were in charge of the ITB, as I recollect, were gentlemen and made me feel humble to the point where to this day, I bow my head in a show of deference to them. My fellow men! I thank you.

Twenty-three companies from seven different countries were made aware of this situation and cooperated once these terms were issued.

The nuclear power plant installation was comprised of the United States' Westinghouse, Combustion Engineering, Canada's AECL, France's Framatome, Germany's KWU, and Japan's Mitsubishi and Hitachi.

Turbines were the forte of the United States' General Electric and Westinghouse, France's Alstom, the United Kingdom's GEC, Japan's Hitachi, Swiss BBC, and Germany's KWU.

The comprehensive design for the nuclear power plants were issued by the United States' Bechtel, Sargent & Lundy, Ebasco, Stone & Webster, Gilbert, France's EDF, and Canada's AECL, and Germany's KWU.

The bidding would start in March 1986, and after a six-month evaluation period, they were going to announce the company which won the bid.

I know I have been talking far too much about technology independence, and yet, in order to achieve this, there were three big hurdles. They include ITB, bid evaluation, and instructions regarding the technique.

We outdid ourselves, and scaled a mountain. The world was surprised by our success. But the next mountain we had to overcome was different. If it is compared to sailing, the ITB is the astronomical observation, which would determine the route, and it would be a lonely sail in a small lake without much wind.

But the bid evaluation would be different. We couldn't do it by ourselves. It was a third-party evaluation. It was not a pleasant thing to be evaluated in the standards of ranks called "*su (Outstanding), wu (Excellent), mi (Good), yang (Average), and ga (Poor)*" but it was not just any evaluation. It was an evaluation that decided the fate of 2 billion dollars. It would not be easy or smooth sailing. There would be hurricanes and big waves.

On this voyage, you could not just rely on your will power, for it would actually rely on external factors. That is why the new business team decided to issue evaluation criteria in advance to ensure fairness.

About six months into the evaluation, on the outside, it looked as if everything was going swimmingly. But underneath the surface, it was loud. All sorts of schemes and maneuvers, and the possibility of spies raged on behind closed doors. The United States, which I considered the foremost authority in the world regarding nuclear power, pushed ahead with its own agenda. Although France was a latecomer compared to the United States, it too, seemed determined to defend what it considered its turf: the South Korean market.

As the tide turned to the United States, domestically, the fight between the Americans grew. During this noisy game, even leading domestic players became involved, and it became a complete mess. Even I, the CEO, was shaken, and I couldn't even envision what my employees must have felt during this time.

I called KEPCO executive Lee Won-bae, along with Lim Han-que, another high-level employee of our company, to my office. I told them, do not be shaken, do not fear, I will shoulder all the responsibility. Security was of the utmost importance. Forget about long-standing ties and lifelong debts. Hadn't everyone known a situation like this would come to pass?

Soon afterwards, Lee came to my office. After ordering coffee, he did not state the reason for his visit. He must be here for a reason, I thought. I broke the silence.

"If you have anything to say, let's hear it," I said.

"Oh, I just came to drink the coffee," he replied. What a dry fellow, I thought to myself. And not befitting to his position, he is pretending that everything's all right. He doesn't know how to lie, however. He is the embodiment of everything that was right (and wrong) from an engineer who had graduated from Seoul National University. He is a straightforward person.

"How perturbed he is! Poor fellow, he is worrying himself to death," I thought.

"Lee, please don't hesitate to speak. Just spit it out," I said.

"The truth is," he said. Then he continued determinedly.

"The long and short of it is that letting the new business development team pick the successful bidder is unrealistic," he said. He wanted to conduct the evaluation according to the CEO's guidelines instead.

"Lee, thank you for your candid advice. However, I promise you that letting the new business development team pick the successful bidder is the right thing to do. There is no way that a third party, even myself, can make such a decision. I promise," I said.

He raised his head and stared at the ceiling for a while. He was a man of few words, to begin with. It was sometimes hard to communicate with him, as he was a little deaf in one ear. He sighed. It was a sigh worth ten phrases, at least. He is at a loss for words, then rises from his seat and leaves the room. From his deep sigh I can tell that he is very worried. I wondered if I was worrying a good man too much. My sympathy for him strikes me to the core.

KEPCO executive Lee must have had a lot of worries. He was a KEPCO veteran of 20-something years. He had also seen KEPCO focus increasingly on nuclear power. There is history, and precedent, and yet, the workers would decide on the successful bidder. This was unheard of. This must have bothered him. CEO Park must be wrong in letting this come to pass, he must have thought.

"President Park must be thinking wrong. He doesn't know the reality, the actual conditions of the work. I must convince him otherwise," he must have thought as he struggled with his conscience all night.

Lee was determined to convince me otherwise, the very next day. He must have been full of thoughts; as they say in Korean, "the Great Wall was built in just one night," as irony. But when meeting with me directly, he had only been able to say a few words and the sigh itself said more than enough.

The truth was, as much as Lee was agonizing over the situation, I myself felt my chest constricting. Until the time came to confirm my correct decision via direct results, there was really no way to make them understand; words were insufficient. But no one wanted to hear or agree with me.

Unfortunately, before the end, I could not win over the gravity of precedent and history. My relationship with Lee soured.

About a month before the evaluation, Lee visited me again in my office. He wore a determined look on his face. He addressed me directly.

"President Park, you have to issue the guidelines by today," he said.

"What do you mean?" I asked.

"Starting from tomorrow, you cross the bridge of no return," he said.

"What bridge? What are you talking about?" I asked.

"We are near the close. You have to make the decision by today! Pick the company you have in mind! If you do not pick, then you cannot redo the evaluation and recalculate the sums," he said.

I suddenly got angry. That he could doubt me, the CEO himself. The compassion I had felt for him suddenly evaporated and was replaced by a type of rage. I hit the desk with my fist.

"Executive Lee, I have said time and time again that as long as I am the CEO, there are no guidelines! Leave my office!" I shouted.

He must have been struck dumb by my sudden anger. He left in a hurry.

To be sure, more than Lee himself, the ones on-site would have felt even more worried. The shape of the successful bidders was coming into view, and without any instructions from above, their anxiety would only grow. If they continued down this path without the big boss designating a particular company, then they would be the ones who would shoulder the burden. The deadline was fixed, so there was no way to recalculate the costs. Executive Director Lee must have been in a bind. He was supposed to convince the CEO; in other words, me.

Six months passed. A lot of words and a lot of (unnecessary) noise. I was also suffering. I lost a lot of friends. Around late September, when the evaluation was at a close, Executive Director Lee came in with the results of the bid evaluation. He wore an expression of great emotion on his face. So the end was here. Finally, his face showed relief and a sense of accomplishment. He displayed a type of confidence that I had never seen before from him.

"President Park, we have the results," he said.

"Wait a minute. Call the other employees in," I said. He looked at me incredulously. He must not have understood.

"Invite them in," I said again.

"Oh, yes," he murmured.

The employees came in. They were full of confidence. Each of them wore a triumphant look on his face. I had done it. We had done it. We had done what others had done in the past, without orders from above. How proud and happy they were. Even I was moved.

"Thank you for your service, gentlemen! As I have promised, I will honor the companies that you yourself have chosen."

I signed the report with a flourish, using one of the Chinese characters for "*jeong*," which in this instance meant, "correct."

The working group had chosen:

- Combustion Engineering (CE) - Primary System 1: NSSS (Nuclear Steam Supply System)
- General Electric (GE) - Secondary System: T/G (Turbine and Generator)
- Sargent & Lundy (S&L) : A/E (Architect Engineering)

We had finally decided on the successful bidders. This was a historic moment.

To my knowledge, it was the first time that the workers, with input from the engineers, picked the companies that they would work with on future projects.

Our picks stunned the international nuclear reactor community. The successful bidders, as well as the ones who lost, were both equally shocked. The results were so unexpected. As they say in the Good Book, those who are proud are humbled, and the humble receive their just due. Our measuring stick had been "who would give us and teach us more of the technology." It appeared as though the ones who had been lobbying the political parties in order to curry favor had failed.

In the past, those who had accepted bribes and such, or promised political kickbacks in exchange for money, had ruled supreme. Even if I paid, I couldn't eat what I wanted, nor get what I wanted. But this time it was different. We did not hesitate in picking what was the best for us, during this pivotal time in history.

What a historic moment, what an epoch-making achievement. Our standards were high and somewhat harsh. We were correct. We had not caved into government demands, or the sweetly scented words of those trying to sway us to pick them. For the first time in KEPCO's history, the engineers on the field had made the final choices on who to work with in the future in the field of nuclear engineering.

Three-Party Contracts

Now the hardest part was over. There was a lot of talk, and unnecessary rumors floating about. Some were extreme. The pushback from the companies that lost, especially the American ones, was severe. They complained that the evaluation was unfair and biased. So from their reasoning, it followed that this evaluation was null and void, and a new one was necessary, and once the new evaluation came through, the technology would be handed down.

"We have worked exclusively with KEPCO for the past 10 years. Right now, we are in the process of building reactor number eight. Do you really want to jeopardize this?"

They were threatening us. It was frightening. They were bullying us, the government as well as the people. We were afraid. Technological independence seemed a goal too far away to reach. We were on the verge of toppling. Was it finally the time to declare the real winner? If we caved, then technological independence would never be achieved. Fine. I had expected this response, somewhat. From the onset, we burnt our boats. There would be no retreat. We were not going to bow down and kowtow, we were going to fight.

The road ahead was long and arduous. Technological independence was our end goal, and we had to overcome this last hurdle. There was no time to waste. Silence was the best defense against unfounded accusations. We had to turn our eyes towards the future. We had already achieved a great goal, so we would have no regrets even if we failed to overcome this last hurdle. Do they not say that for a soldier, the greatest honor is to achieve the target goal then die in battle? This was not a life or death situation anymore.

Stay awake, gentlemen, and tighten the belt around your waist. The fight is not yet over. This is the time to assess the problems at home. The ones who are too ambitious, including our subsidiaries, we have to subdue. The domestic problems themselves may cause greater problems via a rippling effect.

A short time beforehand, there was a fight between the subsidiaries. They wanted a bigger share of the pie. It was a fight that we say in Korean, would decide whose rice bowl would get filled. The biggest problem was the nuclear system design. If we relied on precedent, then the Korea Heavy Industry and Construction (KHIC, or the Doosan Heavy Industries and Construction Co., Ltd. as it is now known) should have been responsible for this job. However, the design work was awarded to the Korea Atomic Energy Research Institute, or KAERI. Both companies lacked the experience. But KAERI had the most amount of brains in Korea. It would come to pass that the nuclear power "hardware," so to speak, would have to be done by KHIC, so if it was also responsible for the System Design, then too many problems would arise behind step two, and too much overlap would arise.

But the opposition to KAERI was great. Fine. They know what the CEO was thinking. The question was, how can we pursue co-management with them, when we were not related, after achieving independence in terms of technology? This was a reasonable assertion. But we could not withdraw our support behind KAERI, especially this late in the game. I had to calm down several different people. I could strike a difficult happy medium that we have a condition that, even though the participation in this Younggwang project, after the technological independence, the technology will be transferred to the relevant party.

To be honest, the general opinion behind assigning this important project to KAERI was akin to a professor starting a business. I could not quell the negative rumors around this assignment. But if you only attempt what is "doable" in this life, then nothing would get done. I had to throw my whole support behind this venture.

Only the Architect Engineering assignment received no censure. Of course, it would be the work of the Korea Power Engineering Company, Inc., or KOPEC (now KEPCO E&C).

Picking the companies to do our bidding is a serious business that unfortunately invites a lot of gossip. I do acknowledge that we fought a lot. We lost a lot of support. Some relationships soured to the point of "crossing the bridge of no return."

But technology independence was a must. We had to abide by the straight and narrow in order to achieve this goal. But the teachers and the students all had problems. The teacher was too well qualified, and the students lagged too far behind.

If I compare this to a marriage, then the marital compatibility sours. To a well-qualified bride, we sent a man with limited means, and because of this, the bride would not be happy. We say in the East, this is the lack of "yúnyǔzhīlè" (雲雨之樂, the physical compatibility between man and woman within a marriage). The bride would only grow in complaints and look for an escape route, as she is about to burst with unhappiness. But even if the sky fell, the marital union would have to stand. We had come this far. We had crossed many mountains and rivers. After indescribable hardships, each family was picked, and an engagement set. How could we break this union?

Because it is a bad family without any connections, without power, without prowess, how many times had it endured humiliation? No matter what happens, this marriage must take place. I'd rather die standing up than sitting, wouldn't you?

A bulldozer is charming and quaint, isn't it? It only gazes ahead and moves forward with a dogged determination. Whether it be trees or rocks, the bulldozer doesn't discriminate. If we are to accomplish anything, let us act like bulldozers.

As per precedent, the main company was KEPCO, and the primary contractors were Korean, and the foreign companies became the subcontractors. They are as follows:

Main Co.	Co. in Charge	Primary Contractor	Subcontractor's Project
KEPCO	KHIC	CE	Making the Machinery of Nuclear Reactor
KEPCO	KAERI	CE	System Design of Nuclear Reactor
KEPCO	KOPEC	S&L	Overall Power Plant Design
KEPCO	KHIC	GE	Turbine & Generator

The technology areas that will be transferred to the Korean primary contractors have been finalized as follows:

Field of Project	Content
Overall Power Plant Design	Sargent & Lundy ▶ KOPEC
System Design of Nuclear Reactor	Combustion Engineering ▶ KAERI
Design of Nuclear Reactor Facilities	Combustion Engineering ▶ KHIC
Turbine & Generator	General Electric ▶ KHIC
Nuclear Fuel	Combustion Engineering ▶ KNFC

The cost of new technology introduction was already in dire straits. It was outside the scope of what the South Korean government had designated for us. KEPCO had to shoulder the cost of what it would take for KAERI and KHIC to learn this new technology. The government official in charge of this operation would need a lot of convincing. But at the same time, KEPCO's strategy wasn't wrong. It was just a lot of difficult situations churning together. The fight would only get bigger from here. We fought a lot. I was standing at the edge of the cliff, and I couldn't budge. Towards the end, we came to a mutual understanding. This difficult fight would be difficult for outsiders to understand. You do not have to understand or empathize with us.

However, if you judge us without knowing the full scope of why we were fighting, and use up a lot of money and mutter excuses, I hope you look at the chart below and repent.

The Cost of New Technology Introduction and Personnel Involved

Field of Project	Co. in Charge	Contractor	Personnel	Cost (KRW)
Making the Machinery of Nuclear Reactor	KHIC	CE	200	25.5 billion
Turbine & Generator	KHIC	GE	120	9.8 billion
System Design of Nuclear Reactor	KAERI	CE	200	83 billion (28 billion + 55 billion)
Overall Power Plant Design	KOPEC	S&L	-	26 billion
Total			520	144.3 billion

*Numbers are approximate.

The nuclear power plant community was surprised. The entire world was surprised. That General Electric and Combustion Engineering would provide the "hardware" for Korean firms? It was an absolute impossibility.

Suffice to say that for example, until just yesterday, General Electric was a cut above KHIC, and many seemed to worship the company. It's not just KHIC that looks up to GE, as the entire world seems to look up to it. That GE had become a subcontractor of KHIC! It was unheard of.

Money is a scary thing. Money makes some people forget about their pride and kneel instead. It's a scary world out there.

We are also anguished. We are doing something out of the ordinary. That a mere student (KEPCO) was now ordering around foreign companies (as their subcontractors) and trying to learn their trade may have been irrational to many. With the need for technology transference, it was a necessary route we had to take, but like I said many times before, it was really pushing the envelope. South Korea would do its best at the helm, but it was inevitable that it would face problems and experience friction.

As soon as we reached the stage of technology transference, people began to talk. You know what I mean. It was noisy with a rising roar of discontent. Combustion Engineering (CE) was especially full of complaints. For them, it must have been very confusing. They had not seen us in such straits before. When they said "KEPCO," they were expecting us to uphold our end of the bargain. But KEPCO was not the one who staged an intervention. We had put KAERI in charge of this part, and they were ivory tower types, who had never done this kind of business. They were awkward and their different practices of course led to friction.

It has been a while now, but even I started worrying about having picked KAERI. They say hindsight is 100 percent, but the surrounding parties were full of complaints. A scientist was a scientist, and not a businessman, they said. They compared it to a priest who loses his job because he lies with a woman; a catastrophe waiting to happen, in other words. That is why there were concerns that KAERI would mess up the business end of things. But I kept pushing back. This was because of Han Pil-soon, Director General of KAERI.

For graduates of the Korea Military Academy (my alma mater), they hold Minister of Science and Techonolgy Kim Sung-jin in high regard. He was a member of KMA Class of 1955, No. 1, and at the top of his class, having graduated summa cum laude.

Once, he had called me to ask a favor.

"CEO Park, if we are to win a Nobel Prize in the near future, then it will be the work of Han Pil-soon. I hope I am leaving him in good hands," he said earnestly. I took Han under my wing. I also pushed him to the brink at times. I heard some curses too. Dear General Kim, we did not win the Nobel Prize, but we have instead created a great businessman in Han.

Our goal was to learn 95 percent of the technology. The remaining 5 percent was a very sensitive issue so it was pushed back so we could deal with it later. But it would not have a huge impact on South Korea achieving nuclear power plant technology independence.

The remaining 5 percent had something to do with the nuclear reactor design code (for example, a PC running Windows instead of a Mac). The three major nuclear power players back then were the United States of America, France, and Japan; but Japan had not learned the design code for itself at that point. And the pump design to circulate the coolant, and the control-measuring device for the nuclear power plant, was unfortunately out of our reach. At that point, it was just too greedy to expect KEPCO to learn this too. If you dine at a Michelin starred restaurant, then after an excellent meal, and after coffee, of course you turn to the best cognac and drink it. This is an act of ignorance, and becoming too big for your britches. Did not Lao Tzu wax lyrical on self-sufficiency?

Even now in the Middle East, KEPCO is in the process of making "perfect" nuclear power plants there.

If I am being totally honest, 95 percent was a high percentage, and a bit greedy of us. It is in the past now, but for experts in the field of nuclear power, they were busy earnestly trying to dissuade me from this target goal and were in favor of lowering it.

Vice President Kim Seon-chang or Yang Chang-gook were old pros; thereby, I listened to their warnings with concern. That I was rushing things. That KHIC, KAERI, and the rest of the companies in South Korea were not ready in terms of experience and skill.

Kim is what I call the "father" of the South Korean nuclear power industry. In 1984 he would be transferred to the Korea Plant Service, or KPS, as the CEO. Before the end of his term at KEPCO, he made sure that our nuclear energy business would continue.

And now we turn to Yang Chang-gook. He was one of the "elites" of South Korea, who had graduated from Seoul National University and also had a master's degree from the University of Oregon. He would later become the CEO at the KEPCO Repair Co., Ltd.

Seasoned pros who have taken care of the project at the management level also shared these concerns. In particular, the PMs, or the Project Managers, at the Kori or Younggwang were on the same page. They are pros. I am an amateur. I was bound to lose confidence.

Now the technology transference caused me to worry a lot. Many experts were concerned about how this would impact our relationship with the United States. But as they say, timing is everything. When I held the flag and hoisted it high, I was already on the brink. To turn back now would be like death. The road ahead was foggy, but I would not die. There was only one way ahead, and that was to keep going.

I remember when the ITB was completed. Everyone had said we wouldn't be able to do it. But Min Kyung-sik's team had pulled it off. KEPCO pulled it off, and preserved our reputation as those who get things done. I became confident. If I had bravery, then the other employees would also feel braver and gain in self-confidence.

There was one other part that I had strongly believed in. This is that KEPCO managed to hire as contractors three companies who were headed by the best of the best, back in the day. These included Korea Heavy Industry's Seong Nak-jeong, KOPEC's Chung Geun-mo, and KAERI's Han Pil-soon. As they say in the East, "Weaklings do not serve a brave general." That is the ultimate truth.

In work, as in all things, do they not talk about timing? We cannot miss this chance. We have to do it, then reap the consequences, as they come. Even if there is only a 51 percent chance of succeeding.

As I had feared, for a while, South Korea's main contractors and the United States' subcontractors kept on fighting amongst themselves. It was a tumultuous time. A fight or two may have been necessary, but this type of friction was concerning. CE stopped working with KAERI and requested to work directly with KEPCO, for example. They said they couldn't stand it. It came to the point where I couldn't let things continue like this.

Unfortunately for KAERI, KEPCO picked its last resort: a systematic three-party contract. For the very difficult phase of technology transfer, which involved "switching on" the nuclear power, KAERI would be the primary contractor, and CE would be the subcontractor, but KEPCO would act as the intermediary between the two. This type of contract is referred to as a tri-party agreement. CE had forced KEPCO's hand. KEPCO had no choice but to yield, so that the business would go smoothly. It was forced, but we're playing by the rulebook.

They had a rather ambiguous and lame title called "a Witness" to deserve the statue, and it did not make a good sense but somehow it turned out to be a solution.

This is because KEPCO played the intermediary, as I have said before. If you do all things with all your heart, then there is a way. There are some scientists who say otherwise, but you cannot fault them. The merchant's way is different from that of a scholar. I am grateful to Han Guk-jong, who handled this matter with wisdom.

The Favored Son

Science and engineering are entirely different, starting from their roots. Science is often irrelevant to how feasible it is from a business and economic standpoint. But engineering is different. Engineering is useless without aligning it with accrued costs.

In the business world, there are certain principles and practices. It's all about bargaining and compromise. It's also about "give and take." A big business does not chase profits alone. It also absorbs damages. There are also ethics used in the business sphere. These rules are not learned easily, but are learned through time and experience.

To learn means to seek the truth. And truth does not sway from one end of the spectrum to another, seeking comfort from whichever side is favorable. A scholar and a merchant cannot be more different from one another. That the two are fighting amongst each other is only natural. It is as if they speak different languages. There are words that are used by scholars, and other words, used by merchants alone. Americans, from my point of view, are ones who are imbued with a sense of ethics whilst conducting business. A scientist's ramblings do not necessarily make sense to a businessman. This is why the vice president of CE, James Veirs, said, "Research and Business must be kept separate." He warned us of this.

When a student commits theft, then the police should arrest the student. The teacher must discipline the student. But the parents should protect the child. That is why each circumstance must fit the bill, so to speak, and adjust to ever varying conditions. This is what we call duty. This is why a person's behavior changes depending on his role. It is only natural that we, the students, who were literally used to a different language, clashed sometimes with the best merchants of the world.

But as time passed, everyone seemed to find his respective role. It is true that even while fighting, "*jeong*," may develop. The scientists and the merchants learned each other's languages, so to speak. KAERI, who was in charge of the system design, was really learning the core technology; it was really difficult work. But our scientists were so talented. That the scientists, with their bright minds, were able to keep up and even outpace them soon made everyone gasp. Even CE was surprised. That is why the Americans must have thought that the South Koreans wouldn't be able to learn it. That we would be able to learn the core technology was beyond their limited understanding of us. They were too foolhardy. We Koreans know.

This is what it was like in the 1980's. This was when we were hit hard with a recession, while Japan was on the rise. Books like *Japan as Number One* or *Japan, the Country Who Can Say No*, were being published. A Japanese conglomerate bought Pebble Beach's golf course, and New York's Empire State Building flew the Japanese flag.

Whenever Japan was ever mentioned, the entire world seemed to be surprised. But whenever South Korea was mentioned, they were lukewarm, bordering on the apathetic. Was it because we were emerging from having been a former occupied country during the Japanese colonial period? But from my view, South Korea surpassed Japan in many respects, even then. Am I going too far?

I know this from personal experience, as a person who endorsed and led the sports world in South Korea. We have more stamina than the Japanese. Just look at Pak Se-ri, Park In-bee. The whole world, not just Japan, is mesmerized by them. Japan knew from the very start that we are a proud and intelligent people. That is why they tried to oppress us sometimes. Because they were afraid.

But the United States doesn't know this. It never foresaw Samsung beating Sony, for example.

The scientists at KAERI, who had learned the tricks of the trade, leapt up and down. An American friend of mine later told me, "When we taught one thing to Koreans, Koreans learned 10."

KEPCO, with a large and generous heart, provided the basic funds, and the new business development team picked the right bride and made sure the marriage took place. During the early days, the marriage was rickety, and things did not go smoothly, but as time passed, things went smoothly thanks to the Korean husband's innate intelligence. A favored son was born.

In the days ahead, due to our nuclear engineering independence, the KSNP-1000 (the Korean Standard Nuclear Plant) was born.

It was like a long march, this technological independence. It was like history was being rewritten. This is due to the hard work of a decade, from KEPCO employees like Kim Seon-chang, Min Kyung-sik, Mun Hee-seong, Lee Jong-hun, Cheong Bo-heon, and their years of experience.

But the curious thing is, how were they able to do this? To give birth to a favorite son that everyone was so proud of?

I am proud of the Koreans of today. And thank you, the United States of America!

On February 17, 2010, KEPCO held a celebratory event in the main auditorium, to commemorate a great achievement; the birth of the first "Nuclear Power Day" in South Korea. It was held to celebrate the export of four APR-1000s (Advanced Power Reactor) to the UAE the year prior. At long last, South Korea became the 5th country in the world to export nuclear power reactors, thereby joining the ranks of the nuclear power plant exporters of the world. This was a momentous occasion. Samsung and LG have long been able to support the South Korean economy. This nuclear power market is alive and well and will survive for years to come. Nuclear Power (and KEPCO) is one of the major companies that will keep our economy's growth engine roaring.

In 2014, the International Energy Agency, IEA, projected that the world's nuclear power capacity would be at 767GW, or 767 Gigawatts of electricity, by 2040. By 2015 standards, the 33 countries in the world that have installed 439 power plants generated, in total, about 377 GW. In the next 15 years, the nuclear energy electricity market will have grown twice-fold.

The APR-1400 is purely a South Korean model. The KSNP-1000 was used as a guide to produce this model. This, again, is a remarkable achievement. When thinking upon it, it feels new. The time it took for us to gain technological independence, ITB, bid evaluation, enterprise selection, and the instruction with regards to the technique… all these things were hurdles that we had to overcome and learn from. But in the end, we prevailed, and now we have created the second, updated version of the KSNP-1000.

To our Korean brethren that have been through all of this through thick and thin, I thank you. You have commanded my full respect.

The APR-1400 took a decade to develop, and took 230 billion won in investment. The number of people behind the project was around 2,000. The head of this business was KEPCO's ace, one of the vice presidents, Shim Chang-saeng. In keeping with the nickname, "Enertopia," he has achieved a great deed.

A core person who made a support was Ahn Byung-hwa, who served as the 10th CEO of KEPCO. He also served as the POSCO CEO and also the Minister of Commerce. He dared to approve an allocation of 230 billion won for R&D. It was not something any Jack and Jill could do.

In the early 1970's, during the early years of the nuclear energy business, we went from a Turnkey model to an Island model, and overcame each new hurdle with the hopes of achieving energy independence. This is how the KSNP-1000 was born. And with the all-South-Korean model, the APR-1400, the big run ended with a big finale. In this battle, however, the top-tier commander died in action. We are all bound to pay a high price to win in a decisive battle. It was a sacrifice to exchange a position and technological independence.

Some people may say that the APR has safety mechanisms in place that are too excessive. Of course the price goes up. But what are really important are the safety protocols and the radiation-leak prevention protocols in place that are worth every penny. We have earned the praise of others as having designed and constructed a "very safe" nuclear power reactor. Do they not have a metaphor in Korea about how if you buy the cheap sticky rice cake just because it's cheap, then you're just wasting your money. You save when you can, and spend when you must.

The six nuclear power reactors currently in operation, the Young-gwang 5 and 6, along with the four reactors of Uljin are currently running smoothly with little to no problems.

Up until recently, South Korea's capability to run the nuclear reactors were on the top level in the world. The nuclear power usage by KEPCO, between the years of 1986 to 1999, was ranked number one 17 times. The average ratio of nuclear power usage in the world was 69.6 percent. South Korea's nuclear power usage was at 87.2 percent, roughly 17 percent higher than the average worldwide. This is equivalent to the economic impact of operating about two extra about 1,000MW nuclear reactors. To even increase the usage by 1 percent saves roughly 40,000 USD. KEPCO's army of men; they have been recognized as some of the best of the best by the world.

There may have been some employees that have not been wise, or messed up sometimes, earning us the censure of the public, but I believe in the Korean people. The ones who will come after us, our descendants, will restore KEPCO's old glory days. I still regret KEPCO's demerger about 10 years ago. When the Korea Hydro & Nuclear Power Co., Ltd. (KHNP) became separate from KEPCO, I believe this may have precipitated the beginning of the end, the first in a series of mistakes. But this is what was predicted, a costly price we had to pay.

KHNP! Be courageous. You are heroes. If you do heroic deeds, then you can become heroes too.

It was a long and arduous journey. Many peoples' sweat and tears went into this, and unfortunately, there are no real records that still stand. By now, shouldn't we have produced a white paper by now? We have no proof behind our blood, sweat, and tears. We have no rare books to show, and appear to be bluffing. Are we just all talk and no action? What will the generations that follow learn from us? After all, we will tell our wartime stories by fireside later. I would like to give a harsh warning, but I decide not to, and I just take a step back in silence.

February 17th, when the first "Nuclear Power Day" in South Korea, there was an Order of Industrial Service Merit clipped to the shoulders of the project head, Shim Chang-saeng. This was only fair.

A reporter there asked him for a comment. Shim gave him a short one.

"Today was only possible because of former South Korean president Chun Doo-hwan, and his full support of nuclear power," he said.

This was recorded in the *50-Year History of KEPCO*.

In truth, without the support of former President Chun, and his original wish for our future, to fuel our energy independence via nuclear power, what we have achieved at KEPCO would not have been possible. We had crossed the "bridge of no return," and accepted no retreat, and will keep on advancing forward until we have achieved our aims. And this is all in thanks to President Chun.

To Continue, or Not, with Nuclear Power

Recently, the accident at Japan's Fukushima Daiichi Nuclear Power Plant has damaged the reputation of nuclear energy around the world. This is a sad aftereffect from my point of view. This accident only fueled anti-nuclear power movements. In Germany, for example, former chancellor Angela Merkel said that eight nuclear power reactors installed before 1990 would be suspended from operating, and by 2022, the last 17 reactors would be suspended. Switzerland also said that its current five reactors still in operation would be phased out by 2034.

Is nuclear energy a bad business? As they simply say sometimes, does it bring about "radioactive dust," and if there is another accident, then does it bring about disaster like the coming of the Anti-Christ?

No, no necessarily. But why would Germany and Switzerland suspend their operations of their thus far well-oiled and currently running nuclear reactors? Should not the Republic of Korea suspend operations of its nuclear power reactors as well?

No, not in my opinion. Yes, it is true that nuclear power plants can cause catastrophe, and bring about "radioactive dust." But why did the United States and the United Kingdom say that they would continue with their support of nuclear power? While Germany and Switzerland have good reasons to suspend their operations of nuclear power, the United States and the United Kingdom also have good reasons to continue their support of it.

This is not a matter of right and wrong, but arises from differences in thought. It is a choice. If I may, I would compare it to boarding a ship to the United States or taking a flight. A flight is faster, but is more dangerous compared to a sea voyage. So the ones who like airplanes will take this route, and the ones who prefer a safer mode of transportation, will select the ship.

Life is a series of choices, small and large. Safety is not 100 percent guaranteed even if you take a "safer" voyage via ship. We all know this, but the safety of the planet itself is guaranteed only by God, in my point of view. Everything boils down to probabilities. Thus, which choice you make, and which will produce the best results, will pervade over one's view of life and one's view of the world.

So from the viewpoint of the Koreans, is it best to continue forward with nuclear energy, or should we stop as well? We should continue. Even if we have to defy risk. Yes. This is my personal viewpoint.

In defiance of risk and fear? Even if we have to risk an accident, like the one that happened in Fukushima? Yes, we must.

In truth, the accident at Fukushima was likely improbable had certain (unfortunate) conditions not taken place. Even in "earthquake paradise" Japan, it was a rare event. In South Korea, this type of accident is almost an impossible probability. I am not saying this without any proof to back my views. For example, in the mid-1970s, an MIT professor named Norman Rasmussen published the "1975 Nuclear Reactor Safety Study." The study states that a nuclear disaster accident, where radioactive effluents spill over, is about once in a million years, according to the scientific statistics of the day. Of course, this study presupposes that the nuclear plant is properly prepared. If Fukushima had established a 15-meter high barrier, then nothing bad would have happened.

On March 3, 2011, a 13-meter high tsunami hit Fukushima. The neighboring Tohoku electric power's Okinawa plant remained safe. All because they had built a 15-meter high wall. In truth, they say that Fukushima is a natural disaster, but I say, it is a man-made one.

The bright minds at Tokyo Electric Power Company Holdings (TEPCO), had concluded that a tsunami over 10-meters high hitting Fukushima was about 0.1 percent, and built the barrier accordingly. They should have built it as high as Tohoku. This was a clever move back then, which backfired, unfortunately.

In truth, Chernobyl and Fukushima's tragedies are man-made disasters that were fully preventable. I am of course not saying that natural disasters are to be treated with little importance. I'm not saying that I'm not afraid of man-made disasters, either. But, if we get properly prepared, we may find a way to stay away from the worst possible scenario, which is a meltdown, with the current level of technology.

Let us return momentarily to the Fukushima power plant disaster. Had TEPCO's CEO told them immediately to start pouring seawater into the reactor, then the disaster would not have been so heartbreaking. I say again, when all factors are taken into account, this was a manmade disaster. But then again, as someone who has headed KEPCO as the CEO,

I wonder if I am being a bit harsh. A nuclear reactor costs at least $400 million USD. Who wouldn't hesitate? I have no confidence either. I would have sank to my knees, as well. However, I am talking from the vantage point of how to "deal with the disaster." Even if Japan had lost hundreds of millions of dollars due to damages, it would have prevented a real disaster by following different protocols. This crisis put them at a crossroads, and the CEO had a really tough decision to make. But had he just screwed his eyes up tight and poured seawater into the reactor, then the disaster would not have been so monumental in scale.

Here, we see a possibility. With our technology and iron will prevent most natural disasters. Nuclear power is not the "Devil." Our current technology and our iron will, as I have stated before, can transform the "Devil" into a "Person."

So as I said before, to continue, or not continue, with nuclear power is a matter of choice. That is why the United States, the United Kingdom, and even Japan have chosen to continue using electricity generated by nuclear power.

We Koreans have gotten the all-clear. "Go." This is an excellent choice, from my point of view.

It's easy to say that we will be environmentally friendly by embracing other types of alternative energy. But we are far from achieving this goal. Wind power and solar power have a long way to catch up. By KW, when comparing the amount of electricity produced by the aforementioned alternative energies, it becomes all too clear that they are not as efficient. Coal costs 71 won, LNG 126 won, water power 118 won, oil 150 won, wind power 124 won, and solar power 264 won per KW (as of this writing). But nuclear power costs 62 won per KW.

Our neighboring Japan's Fukushima accident stunned us all. From a different vantage point, many mass media outlets printed news that were unfavorable towards nuclear energy. There was no persuading some of them. That is fine. This is my belief, to this day. So some might ask me, "How are your beliefs in nuclear energy so sound?" Fine. I will now bring up Bill Gates, the American co-founder of Microsoft and a philanthropist to boot. Gates visited South Korea in 2013, as many of you will remember.

He visited the Blue House, and one of the most important talking points he brought up was the 4th generation of nuclear power. It was about a year after the Fukushima disaster. After hearing him speak, then-South Korean President Park Geun-hye agreed wholeheartedly with him and decided to develop it in connection with what South Korea has called the "creative economy."

So what was Gates developing? In 2006, he established and founded a company called TerraPower, which is in charge of building a Traveling Wave Reactor (TWR), a type of sodium-cooked fast reactor (SFR). So why is a genius like Gates focusing on nuclear power? He has judged after being a part of creating cutting-edge technologies, that the anti-nuclear movement that many hold, along with human errors, and even the by-products produced by nuclear power, all pale in comparison to the benefits of nuclear power. In his view, nuclear power is the safest and the most environmentally friendly option that is currently available.

Of course, the type of nuclear power he is currently developing is somewhat different. The type he is developing now is, compared to current standards, cheaper, smaller, and safer. There is no reason to enrich the fuel, and no need to recycle used raw materials, and as I stated before, it is smaller (width 3 m, length 4 m). As they are smaller in size, they can be buried in the land and still can function for a century. The U.S. government has also taken interest in this venture, going as far as to invest $850 million dollars under the Obama administration. Is South Korea also not a nuclear (energy) power? We have also birthed world-class scientists, that is why Gates was so interested in us and asked us for help. Handong University's President, Chang Soon-heung, is interested in this project, and KEPCO's nuclear development office were also supposed to work with them; alas, the project has stalled due to some conditions that they couldn't agree on. Do you see why I still fully support nuclear power? It is not without its merits.

In life, there are times when one meets a crossroads. A person's attitude towards life and how he copes with the world can be divided largely into two groups: those who are active and those who are passive. You can also say some are conservative while some others are more progressive. But again, attitudes and possibilities are a consequence of thoughts.

What do I mean by this? In life, "nothing is for free." When we think upon it, the animal kingdom exists; carnivores kill to eat. That life is sustained by killing is a rule of nature, and of the world. Like I said, "nothing is for free."

When you are at a crossroads, one path may be filled with danger. Most people will avoid this dangerous route. But the right choice is often the dangerous one. If one doesn't endure risk, then what will you earn in return? In this world, where nothing is for free, what do the laws of Nature dictate?

The world explains how Samsung outpaced Sony via all sorts of theories. But when you look carefully, the key to Samsung's success was to use reasonable methods. One of these was risk taking.

Risk taking can prop up an organization or even lead to national prosperity. Risk taking involves bravery to reach/stay at the top, then relies on the employees and the citizens of the nation. When danger is ahead, opportunity comes. To be courageous and not lose bravery, to not avoid the competition but to face it head on, this is when an organization is filled with a fighting spirit. An organization becomes full of tension, but unifies under this tension. When an organization is at a crossroads, if you, as an individual, shirk your duty, then it will contribute to the decline of the organization.

Only the fittest survive, and/or, the theory of natural selection abides. The rules of the universe are actually the result of natural laws, or logic, governing Heaven as well as Nature. A person who is talented barges ahead, and competition ensures that there will be a pecking order. The liberal left may say that communism works, but I say that without competition, the world would be left in chaos. Why do you think communism failed, by most accounts?

By some accounts, nuclear power can bring about disaster. But our current technology is so safe that we are sure to avoid a nuclear meltdown. Are you going to not make soybean paste because you are afraid of flies? Remember, lads, nothing in this life is for free.

This is the lesson that we must learn about nuclear power.

To Resign, or To Not

In July 1987, Kim Jong-chae, the Director of Construction, sought my approval over a contract. It was shortly after we announced the winning bidders for the 11 and 12 nuclear reactors.

"What do I have to sign this time?" I asked.

"A private contract with Hyundai," he said impassively.

"What do you mean, this is the construction business. They have to bid, just like the rest of them," I said.

"It's a public work, henceforth, it must be with Hyundai," he said.

"What a stalwart fellow," I thought to myself. And to say that it must be a private contract, and his cheeks didn't even flush red.

"A public work, Hyundai, private contract, I don't understand," I said. "Since it is a publicly-funded work, of course they must bid, just like the rest of them," I said.

"Oh, did you not know?" he asked.

"Know what," I asked.

"Well, as the Fates would have it..."

To summarize, basically, Kim said that the nuclear power plant must have an ASME (American Society of Mechanical Engineers) Stamp issued to them, and the only conglomerate with this certification was Hyundai. That is why for the past 10 years, this project had been with Hyundai, thanks to an exclusive, private contract.

He made it sound as if without Hyundai, nothing could be done. He wrapped his favorite conglomerate around his metaphorical arms. I found out later that to him, it was so cut and clear that he was unable to understand why I was flustered and upset.

"Ok, ok. Let's do it." I signed the contract.

Kim Jong-chae. A graduate of the College of Engineering at Seoul National University, his wealth of knowledge and brilliant, logical mind always moved me, almost to tears. Once, he had refused to be promoted, along with Kim Jae-sup, another chief of yet another department. They didn't want the executive director titles.

"Why are you declining a promotion?" I asked.

"Well, I can't accept it," he said.

"Do you have a good reason for declining?" I asked.

"It's simply not my time. There are older, more senior employees that should be above me," he said.

"What a tremendous fellow," I thought to myself. He seemed larger than life to me after that incident. While he had mentioned the private contract to me, and his resolve was resolute I didn't really feel a lot of resentment towards him in the end because he had earned my respect.

Maybe a month passed. A government official issued a notice that we had to nullify the contract with Hyundai.

"What nonsense is this?" I thought.

I made a phone call to the Ministry of Trade, Industry, and Energy. I spoke to the head himself.

"Minister, we cannot cancel the contract this late in the game," I said.

"It's a private contract, so why can't you cancel it?" he asked languidly.

"This is not your normal type of private contract," I said.

"What's different about it?" he asked rudely.

"Our nuclear power plants need the ASME certification, which only Hyundai has, which is why Hyundai has been in this line of work for 10 years," I said.

"Well, our government says this is a no-go. Cancel it," he ordered.

"What kind of absurdity is this!" I lost my temper.

"Minister, I cannot do what you ask," I said.

"What? What are you saying?" he asked crankily.

"We had an agreement, a private contract with Hyundai, and this contract is flawless. How can we terminate an agreement one-sidedly?" I heard anger in my voice.

"President Park. These are direct orders, straight from the government. Cancel it," he said.

I held the phone for a long time after that. I breathed in and out. I was furious. Yes, I am the CEO of KEPCO, and I could not abide by his bullying. I just held the phone at arm's length.

"President Park, President Park…" The Minister sounds mad.

"As I have stated before, Minister, I cannot cancel the contract. I'd rather resign than sign the new paperwork," I said. I hung up.

He called me back. I didn't pick up my phone.

I ran and went into the Minister's office right away. I placed my letter of resignation on his desk.

"I do apologize," I said. No more words were necessary.

I turned away, and began to walk away. And what's this! The Minister has me by the arm. I think it's rude to leave like this. I pretended I couldn't be overcome by him, and reluctantly sat.

The tea was brought in. I didn't have much to say. The Minister doesn't have much to say either. We sat in stony silence.

Choi Chang-rak, Seoul National University graduate, and he had studied Economics at Vanderbilt University, in Nashville, Tennessee. He was a good-looking man, and reminded me of the *seonbi*, or a Korean scholar from years past. I learned a lot from him. From my days at Korea Heavy Industries and Construction Co Ltd., he had helped me from his position as the head of the Korea Development Bank. Today was a sad day indeed.

I stopped by the press office. A journalist is a reporter, not for nothing. Several of them soon convened. Questions burst forth from their lips. I didn't feel like pontificating, and there was really no need to, either.

"Several days ago, I approved a private contract that I was wary of, and was ordered to cancel the contract today. This makes me look like a snake in the grass. In business, there are laws, and a contract is a binding promise. I have an upper hand on the hierarchy, but then, if I cannot keep a promise, it is only natural for me to resign.

I rose from my seat. Several of the reporters swarmed around me. I ignored them. When I returned to KEPCO, I ordered chief officer Lim to pack my things.

To make a long story short, my successor, Han Bong-su, canceled the contract with Hyundai. After a few days, he re-approved it and signed a private contract with Hyundai. This was not a laughing matter. This is how business is conducted in South Korea.

Two Hundred Employees Parrot the Same Thing

And pretty soon, Roh Tae-woo became president of the Republic of Korea. He was part of the 6th Republic. The 5th Republic, which harbored the likes of me, began to fall under his direction. To draw out the successor's misdeeds and tarnish his image, is all the new group of government officials wanted to do. This is stupidity, in my point of view. Even for low-ranking politicians. This is a political scheme. We still have not achieved mastery of politics, so no wonder why this process after a new one is inaugurated is always the same. What a shame.

They even came up with a nickname for us: "The Corruption of the 5th Republic." To them, the easiest target was the nuclear power plant business. They thought if they shake us, then something was bound to fall out. I, the former CEO of KEPCO, became the target.

It began with the Board of Audit and Inspection. The largest audit team that I had ever seen by that time came in for an all-inclusive inspection of the premises. The regular day-to-day operations of KEPCO seemed paralyzed; that's how exacting and thorough, and intense it was. They searched high and low for three months. The employees' pain was indescribable.

Most of the events that happened under my tenure were placed on a type of chopping block. From the 11 and 12 nuclear reactors, from the bidding wars to the inspection and contract signing they examined very closely. This was because Westinghouse took an issue with the 11th and the 12th reactors and even demanded the deals nullified. The official report was hundreds of pages long. But they found nothing to censure us about. No one was harmed, and no one was axed. The inspectors from the nation's top auditing agency found objectively that fairness and proven results regarding reactors 11 and 12. Westinghouse's protests were silenced, ironically, thanks to these thorough men.

And now the prosecutors came in. They wanted to discuss reactors 11 and 12 and the legality of it. About 200 employees were called in to testify for a month. Lim Han-que, Shim Chang-saeng, actually started their workdays by heading to the Public Prosecutor's Office for a full month.

Two hundred employees strong said the same thing. All of them said the same thing. "The CEO did not make us do it, we did it ourselves." A month passed.

This heated investigation was supposed to expose the underbelly of the company to "expose the real truth." The only ones who were disappointed were some businessmen who were looking to work with the current government. As they say in Korea, "there was a great deal of fuss, but not much came of it."

One day, the prosecutors summoned me. The prosecutor in charge of my investigation was Chung Sang-myung. He would eventually rise to the position of Prosecutor General of South Korea.

"It's a curious thing. Two-hundred something employees all keep on saying the same thing. I wonder if they had started putting their stories together before the investigation. They really impressed me," he said.

I laughed. He laughed with me too.

The Grand Finale

And now I come to the part I have been hesitant to write about. It may be thoughtless of me, and some may say it's a false story that may cause me to become a laughingstock. The people around me whined. That truths have to be left in writing, as a report of sorts. It is a type of calling. If I were afraid of finger pointing, then I should not have been on the national stage for anything, or so they implied.

Some men try to shove Herodotus down other's throats, and even refer to the ancient Chinese classics, *Records of the Great Historian* (*Shiji*) and *Book of Document* (*Shujing*). Did you forget how inspiring *The Odyssey* was?

I am now eighty, and cannot put it off for longer.

I wrote this in a hurry, so I did not use caution whilst writing. It may be rough in parts. The parts I got wrong, the harsh language, I ask for your patience and understanding.

While I was resting at home, I had no regrets. Everything was my fault, and not others'. If I had just sat in the CEO's office, in the CEO's chair, twirling and doing nothing, then I would have had no reason to fight. This may have been God's will. KEPCO was sure to have historical repercussions. I would say that maybe it is the "*Cheonmyung*," or God's will, at work here. I had no choice but to submit my resignation. Everything in this life is a series of causes and effects, and with everything, I can say that I did my best. That is why Enertopia is at hand, and the technology independence was achieved. These were my long cherished hopes.

On July 16, 1987, the employees gathered at the new office headquarters' courtyard. All the others who worked elsewhere for KEPCO watched from their TV screens. They were gathered to see my sending-off ceremony.

The public relations manager, Park Won-tae, who had always had warnings as well as advice to dispense, had prepared a farewell speech that was thick with pages. I glanced through it. It was excellent. But too long. I did not wish to speak so many words. I advanced to the podium. I drew a long breath.

Slowly, I began my farewell speech.

"Nature gives humanity good rules to abide by. Whilst we speak of a bubbly brook, a deep river flows without sound. The wind may rustle through the trees, but the wind that passes over a mountain ridge has no sound. My beloved KEPCO brothers and sisters, goodbye!"

July 2014

Eugene

APPENDIX

Photos

The Course of My Life in KEPCO
Apr. 1983 to Sept. 1987

“Communication” (Mt. Halla, 1986.5.10.)

"Special Lecture on Behavioral Codes and Modes of Conduct" (1983.11.15.)

"KEPCO's Southern Rally" (Nogodan Peak, 1985.5.11.)

Kim Jae-jin, head of the North Gyeongsang Province, and Park Man-yun, head of the South Jeolla Province, hang a commemorative gold medal around my neck. (1985.5.11.)

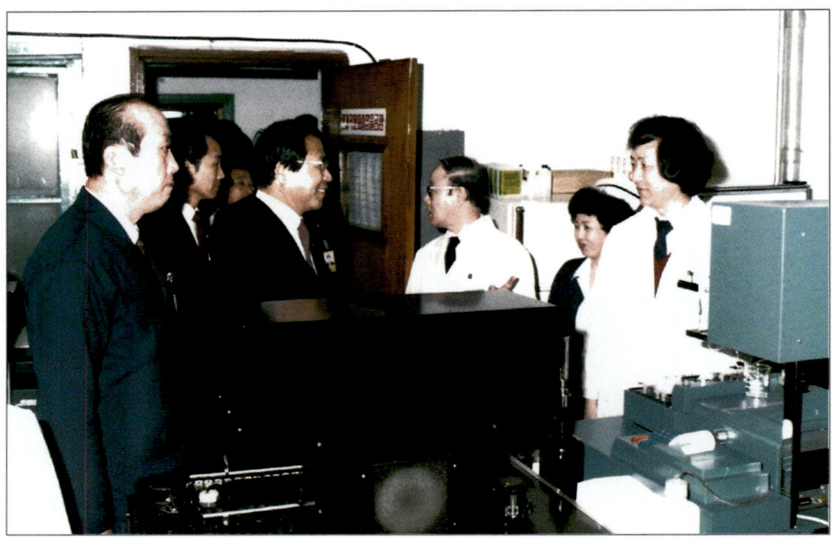

Hanil General Hospital Inspection (1985.1.17.). From the left, hospital director Noh Tae-il, executive director Min Kyung-sik, me, and other hospital staff.

A dedication ceremony for an apartment building for KEPCO employees in Ssangmun-dong (1986.11.20.)

Sejong Center for the Performing Arts, the First Kyunghyang Shinmun's Grand Prize in Energy (1985.10.8.)

Panorama of the Sokcho Living and Training Institute in Aug. 1987 (KEPCO broke ground on this project in 1985)

The KHNP Human Resources Development Institute (formerly known as the Kori Training Institute). In March 2012, the KEPCO International Nuclear Graduate School (KINGS) was established. Over 55 students from 19 countries, along with South Korean students, make up a student body of around 120.

에너토피아의 태양

물거든
에너지의 태양이라고 말하라.
해 뜨는 동해
고리 언덕에
민족의 자존의 불꽃이
힘차게 타오르기 시작했다.
찬란히 뻗어가라
이 우렁찬 힘의 동맥이여.
여긴 시작이 있을 뿐
끝은 처음부터 마련되지 않았다.
전력은 국력이고
겨레 생존의 길이라
그러나 에너지의 자원이 부족한 나라
이에 한국전력공사가
하늘같은 의지와 바다같은 힘으로
기어이 세워낸 원자력 발전소
1호기 2호기
5호기 6호기
시작이 장했으니
최대의 결실이 또한 여기에 있어라.
가슴 가슴에 새겨두라.
우리의 지혜들이 크게 이바지한
5.6호기
영롱하게 정화됐다고.
어제의 수평선이
오늘 우리들의 날개 밑에 머문다.
이 건설에 쏟은 헤아릴 수 없는 땀과
모든 자재는 [illegible]하지 않으리
다만 나라 중흥의 불길이
민족의 번영과 함께
영원히 꽃피어 있으리라고.

시 황금찬
글씨 김구용

A poem dedicated to Enertopia. Written by Hwang Geum-chan, a South Korean poet, and inscribed by Kim Gu-yong.

A commemorative large boulder at Kori, titled, *Enertopia* (1986.6.2.)

The "1st KEPCO National Youth Football Tournament" (Chungju, 1984.10.26.)

Triple Crown winner Lim Chun-ae, at the 10th Asian Games 1986 Seoul

Official headquarters of KEPCO at Gangneung. Construction began on May 1, 1988, and was completed on September 24, 1990.

A panoramic view of Gangneung headquarters. On the left, Myeongryedang, center, Changsingak, and on the right, Gwangyeongru.

A monument dedicated to Wolseong Nuclear Reactor 1, number 1 in the world in terms of efficiency (1986.3.3.)

Jeonju company building. Broke ground in 1983, completed on December 5, 1985. Currently the Jeonbuk Official Headquarters.

Seoul National University professor Kim Jin-gyun's masterpiece, KEPCO's Gwangju headquarters. Currently Gwangju/South Jeolla Province HQ. Finished on May 26, 1990.

Gyeongju HQ. Broke ground on December 19, 1986. Completed on March 31, 1989.

Pine tree garden with *Love for Mankind*, the sculpture by Hongik University Professor Choi Ki-won.

Panoramic view of Samseong-dong's KEPCO headquarters.

Seoul National University professor Lim Song-ja's masterpiece, the *Statue of the KEPCO Employee*. Located in the pine tree grove at the official KEPCO headquarters.

Dynamism. An exhaust pipe transformed into sculpture. A joint project of professors Kim Young-joong and Kwon Soon-hyung.

Me embracing the Bechtel CEO, on his visit to South Korea on December 15, 1983. I am on the right.

Nuclear Power Engineering leaders: From the left, Han Guk-jong, vice deputy head, Shim Chang-saeng, deputy head, Choi Dae-yong, deputy head, Kim Jong-chae, deputy head, Lee Jong-hun, vice president, me, Park Chun-geo, auditor, Lee Won-bae, executive, Jang Gi-ok, deputy head, Lim Han-que, deputy head.
Not pictured: Executive director Min Kyung-sik, Chung Geon, deputy head, and Lee Joong-jae, vice deputy head.